Is Peaceful Coexistence Possible Between Christians and Muslims?

*An attempt to bring believers of both
faiths to embrace a peaceful
and amicable relationship*

Samir Moura

Grosvenor House
Publishing Limited

This book is published by
Grosvenor House Publishing Ltd
Link House
140 The Broadway, Tolworth, Surrey, KT6 7HT.
www.grosvenorhousepublishing.co.uk

A CIP record for this book
is available from the British Library

ISBN 978-1-80381-216-8
eBook ISBN 978-1-80381-217-5

CONTENTS

CONTENTS

CONTENTS

FOREWORD

Our goal in this book is to examine the possibility for Christians and Muslims of different sects to live side by side peacefully and in harmony, in the light of a new open-minded reading of the Bible and the Koran, based on recent interpretations and new logical thinking, taking into account the considerable development of sciences since the advent of these two religions, the progress made by humanity since then and the needs for religious groups to cooperate and deal with each other in this era of globalization. We should not forget that as all sides are believers in One Merciful God, God cannot but wish for his believers from either side to come closer and compromise.

PREFACE

The killing, destruction and horrors of the civil wars in Syria, Iraq and the Middle East, where tens of thousands of innocent people are being killed due to their religious beliefs, Yazidi women plundered and sold in slave markets, whole cities destroyed, tens of thousands of people with amputated limbs unable to work in need of care, millions of orphaned children, old women and men trying to find a shelter and a crust of bread, where the historic remains of the old civilizations of Assyria, Greece and Rome are being destroyed by the Islamic State and Al-Qaeda's barbarians, pushed me, an ex-resident of the martyred city of Aleppo, to write this book about the madness of religious fanaticism, that transformed human beings into the worst types of beasts.

The Author

Note: This book was translated to English by the Author who wrote the book originally in Arabic.

Chapter One

The development of religious thought in the Ancient Near East

Knowledge of God developed with time, as men even in prehistory strived to understand the reason for their existence and the forces that controlled it. With the dawn of history at the beginning of the forth millennia BC (Before Christ), we find from archaeological excavations in cuneiform writing the development of religious thought of the peoples of Mesopotamia. The Sumerians believed in many gods, each god controlling certain natural phenomena, and each town with its own supreme god. Later, the Akkadians as well as the Amorites, Babylonians and Assyrians believed in the supremacy of their own single god over all the other gods. In addition to their beliefs in many gods, these peoples developed religious and secular laws for their societies, the most renown being the Code of Laws of the Babylonian King Hammurabi (ruled from about 1792 to 1750 BC) who first came up with "an eye for an eye and tooth for a tooth" formula (Law 196 & 200).

His Code of Laws also covered social and commercial relationships: The slave to be liberated after four years (Law 117: If a man be in debt and sell his wife, son or daughter,... for three years they shall work in the house of their purchaser or master; in the fourth year they shall be given their freedom.), while in Moses' Law, it was after seven years (Exodus 21,2). A thief had to return tenfold the amount of stolen goods (Hammurabi Law 8: If a man steal ox or sheep, ass or pig... he shall render tenfold), while in Moses' Law, he could be killed if he is caught stealing or had to return two times the amount (Exodus 22:1–3) and Hammurabi's Law punished judges who accepted bribes (Law 5 & 33) while Moses' Law just forbade corruption (Exodus 23: 2 & Deuteronomy 16: 18–19). Hammurabi's Code of Laws was the first written law in History (Robert W. Rogers, The Code of Hammurabi, New York 1917/ The Avalon Project – Documents In Law, History & Diplomacy – The Code of Hammurabi, Translated by L.W. King).

Also, the peoples of Mesopotamia, starting with the Sumerians wrote in cuneiform script on clay tablets the stories and myths between men and gods, the most famous being the Sumerian mythical *Epic of Gilgamesh* translated later to Akkadian language (around 1900 BC). It told about the will of the gods to punish men for their sins by sending a destructive flood similar to the one we find in the Bible (the story of Noah) in most of its details but with the gods now replaced with a single God.

The Ancient Egyptians also worshiped a multitude of gods. Some of those gods were considered more important than others, like the god of the afterlife Osiris, the god Horus son of Osiris that was consolidated with that of Amon-Re the sun god, of whom the Pharaoh came to be regarded as the incarnation, and his consort the goddess Isis. For a short period, the Pharaoh Akhenaton (died around 1336 BC) tried to replace the worship of multiple gods with that of a single god: Aton (the sun god) but the priests rose against him and after his death, returned to polytheism. The Ancient Egyptians believed that each god controlled a specific natural phenomena and they believed that the Pharaohs were of divine origin and accordingly they worshipped them as gods. They built grandiose temples to these gods to obtain their favours. The Ancient Egyptians believed in the resurrection of the dead in body and soul, and afterlife judgment before Osiris, where good and bad people would meet their just reward. To preserve the body of the dead, they embalmed it and placed it in impressive underground tombs and grandiose above ground pyramids.

Prophet Abraham's Semitic tribe, which moved with its flocks from the Sumerian town of Ur (in southern Mesopotamia) to Harran (northern Mesopotamia), where Abraham came to believe in a single God, and from where he was commanded by God to leave his pagan tribe (around 1900 BC) and move to the land of Canaan, the Promised Land, where he and his descendants lived until the sons of his grandson Jacob, with their youngest brother Joseph, moved to Egypt due to a famine that struck the land of Canaan. They lived in Egypt for many generations until they rebelled against the tyranny of Egypt's Pharaoh, and under the leadership of the son of a Levite: Moses, who was adopted and raised by the daughter of the Pharaoh according to the Bible (Exodus 2: 1–10), upholding their belief in a single God, escaped from Egypt to Canaan. The date of their escape might have taken place sometime after the death of Akhenaton – the Egyptian Pharaoh, and the rebellion of the Egyptian army and priests against the imposed by him worship of Aton (the single sun god). The Hebrews after forty years spent in the Sinai desert and the land of the Midianites crossed the river Jordan and entered the land of Canaan under the leadership of Eshoo the assistant of Moses, whereby comes their name "Hebrews" meaning the "ones who crossed". The Hebrews after many battles with the Canaanites and other peoples inhabiting the land of Canaan established according to the Bible, kingdoms in parts of this land: King David (ruled from about 1010 till 970 BC) and Solomon (from about 970 till 930 BC).

During this long period of wandering from Mesopotamia to Canaan to Egypt and through the contacts they established with the peoples of these countries and their religious beliefs, the patriarchs, the wise men and the prophets of the Hebrews (starting with Abraham) came to believe in a single God creator of the universe and life. The most distinctive features of His cult were that no image was to be made of Him, that He is invisible and that He made man in his own image. These features made him totally different from the supreme gods of Mesopotamia and Egypt. The Hebrews reached their belief in a single God after rejecting all that seemed illogical to them in the beliefs of these peoples, and probably by the grace of God. To Abraham and his descendants befall this favour. This favour is mentioned in the Koran (Surah 2: 47:"O children of Israel! Remember My favour where-with I favoured you and how I preferred you to all creatures").

The accumulation of the beliefs of the Hebrews (the Children of Israel, as the sons of Jacob came to be called), their prophets and wise men from Abraham and up to the 5th Century BC, allowed the writing of the five books (Pentateuch: Genesis, Exodus, Leviticus, Numbers and Deuteronomy) of the Torah in their final form, as collected by the scribe Ezra after the Hebrews return from the Babylonian exile. Although all classical Jewish rabbinic views hold that the five books were entirely or almost entirely Mosaic and of divine origin, in them we find traces of the Hebrews years of captivity in Babylon with the old myth of Gilgamesh and the Code of Laws of Babylonian king Hamurabi. The Hebrew bible (Tanakh, also known as Mikra, meaning 'reading'. Similar to the meaning of 'Karan' in Arabic) as well as the Old Testament of the Christians includes besides the five books of the Torah, the Book of the Prophets and the Writings. The Book of the Prophets consists of the books of Joshua, Judges, Samuel, Kings, Isaiah, Jeremiah and Ezekiel as well as the books of the twelve Minor Prophets. The Writings consist of eleven books: The Psalms, Proverbs, Job, The five books of the Song of Songs, the Book of Ruth, the Book of Lamentations, Ecclesiastes, the Book of Esther, Daniel, Ezra–Nehemiah and Chronicles. The Hebrew Bible according to some scholars didn't take its final form until the first century AD in Palestine.

Chapter Two

The Hebrew Bible and the Law of Moses

From the times preceding Christ, no more important book reached us as is the Hebrew Bible. Some other literary works from the old civilizations of the Near East did reach us from recent archaeological excavations but none reached us through ancient manuscripts as the Hebrew Bible. The Hebrew Bible over the centuries went through many phases of auditing and authentication before it took its present form. There were many teachers beside historians who participated in writing the Hebrew Bible, expressing the words of the legislator in the person of the Prophet Moses, in whose mouth spoke Jehovah (God), and the words and teachings of the prophets who followed him. Of the teachers who participated in writing the Bible were the wise men. Unlike Moses' Law, emanating according to Hebrew rabbis from God, Wisdom originated from men. The renowned books of Wisdom were those of Job and the Proverbs. The goal of these teachers was the development of ethics, justice, social well-being during life on Earth and not the saving of one's soul. The prophet held a particular position between the teachers, and the Hebrew faith begins with the prophets.

As described above, the founders of the Hebrew beliefs were nomads (Abraham, Isaac, Jacob, to name a few) and their traditions and way of life were similar to the way of life of other Semitic peoples amongst whom they lived in Mesopotamia and in the Land of Canaan. The Prophet Jacob and his ancestors were wandering Arameans (Deuteronomy 26: 5: "Then you shall declare before the Lord your God: My father was a wandering Aramean, and he went down into Egypt with a few people and lived there and became a great nation, powerful and numerous"). Their contacts with the Egyptian civilization enriched their beliefs without much changing their way of life and customs as a nomadic people. Before their entry to Egypt, the Hebrew patriarchs, starting with Abraham, had already established a covenant with God, who promised them to multiply their descendants and to give them as inheritance the Land of Canaan.

Prophet Moses had a major influence on the religious beliefs of the Hebrew people. The ten commandments of Jehovah (God) written on stone tablets and kept in the tabernacle are the basis of the Hebrew Bible. At Mount Sinai, Jehovah spoke to Moses from a fire (Deuteronomy 5: 4–21) giving him a promise He will keep as long as the Children of Israel (the Hebrews) stay faithful to Him.

It was Moses who saved his people from slavery and led them out of Egypt, but was not allowed to enter the promised land due to a sin he committed (Exodus 32: 19, Numbers 27: 12–14), (The Koran, Surah 28: 15–16, Surah 7: 150–151).

The Ten Commandments of God (Deuteronomy 5: 6–21) are thought to be the ethical basis of all later man-made legislations. Below we provide them as listed in the English Standard Version (ESV):

1. "I am the Lord your God, who brought you out of the land of Egypt, out of the house of slavery. You shall have no other gods before me.
2. You shall not make for yourself a carved image, or any likeness of anything that is in heaven above, or that is on the earth beneath, or that is in the water under the earth. You shall not bow down to them or serve them; for I, the Lord your God, am a jealous God, visiting

the iniquity of the fathers on the children to the third and fourth generation of those who hate me, but showing steadfast love to thousands of those who love me and keep my commandments.

3. You shall not take the name of the Lord your God in vain, for the Lord will not hold him guiltless who takes his name in vain.

4. Observe the Sabbath day, to keep it holy, as the Lord your God commanded you. Six days you shall labour and do all your work, but the seventh day is a Sabbath to the Lord your God. On it you shall not do any work, you or your son or your daughter or your male servant or your female servant, or your ox or your donkey or any of your livestock, or the sojourner who is within your gates, that your male servant and your female servant may rest as well as you. You shall remember that you were a slave in the land of Egypt, and the Lord your God brought you out from there with a mighty hand and an outstretched arm.

5. Honour your father and your mother, as the Lord your God commanded you, that your days may be long, and that it may go well with you in the land that the Lord your God is giving you.

6. You shall not murder.

7. And you shall not commit adultery.

8. And you shall not steal.

9. And you shall not bear false witness against your neighbour.

10. And you shall not covet your neighbour's wife. And you shall not desire your neighbour's house, his field, or his male servant, or his female servant, his ox, or his donkey, or anything that is your neighbour's".

Besides the Ten Commandments, Moses (or could it be later the rabbis?) did add many other rules and regulations to be followed by the Israelites. These included prayer rituals, the sacrifice of animals, allowable meat to consume (specific to animals on land, sea and air), the rituals for ablutions before prayers and other hygiene rules, the methods to be used to diagnose illnesses and to recover from them (leprosy and others). It included also the mercy to show towards fellow Israelites, which included dispensing them of debt payment after the passage of seven years, the approach to follow with foreign peoples (obligation of capital and interest payment for loaned money), and in general their relations with the peoples surrounding them.

The Law of Moses (the Torah) as collected by the scribe Ezra after the Hebrews return from the Babylonian Exile was in fact a secular constitution, amalgamating the Mosaic Ten Commandments of God with the traditions of a tribal society, certain Babylonian mythological stories and rules based on Hamurabi's Law, as well as some beliefs and traditions of the settled Egyptian people. It provoked a cultural revolution which brought the cultural level of the Israelite tribes to a much higher level, and allowed them to impose their rule on the surrounding desert tribes and peoples.

We find in the Torah the first mention of the tribute to be imposed on conquered peoples (Deuteronomy 20: 10–14: "When you draw near to a city to fight against it, offer terms of peace to it. And if it responds to you peaceably and it opens to you, then all the people who are found in it shall do forced labour for you and shall serve you. But if it makes no peace with you, but makes war against you, then you shall besiege it. And when the LORD your God gives it into your hand, you shall put all its males to the sword, but the women and the little ones, the livestock, and everything else in the city, all its spoil, you shall take as plunder for yourselves. And you shall enjoy the spoil of your enemies, which the LORD your God has given you.")

The mention of tribute in the Koran came 2000 years later (Surah 9: 29: "Fight against those who have been given the scripture who do not believe in Allah and the Last Day, and forbid not that which Allah has forbidden by his Messenger, and follow not the Religion of Truth, until they are compelled to pay the tribute readily, being brought low").

As these rules were thought to be coming from God, they couldn't evolve with time, as did man-made laws and constitutions of other peoples, which evolved with time through acquired experience, accumulated knowledge and social progress.

Besides the Law of Moses (the Torah), the Hebrew Bible contains a detailed description of the history of the Israelites up to the Babylonian exile and beyond, and the biography of the Israelite prophets and their teachings along with that of their kings and described these as humans prone to commit sin and to repent.

The prophet Amos was the first to ascribe to Jehovah the quality of a God for all humanity (Amos 9: 5–7) and not a God only for the tribe of Israel. The prophet Isaiah confirmed the sanctity of God and revealed His perfection, and spoke about the advent of the Messiah – the Prince of Peace whose reign and authority will prevail worldwide, and under his rule people will convert their swords and pikes into ploughshares, and wolves will live with sheep (Isaiah 2: 2-4, and 11: 1–9).

An obvious shortcoming of the Torah is the Israelites belief that they are the only people chosen by God (Deuteronomy 14: 2: "For you are a people holy to the LORD your God, and the LORD has chosen you to be a people for his treasured possession, out of all the peoples who are on the face of the earth."), and the unequal status which it established between them and the other peoples (Deuteronomy 15: 6: "For the LORD your God will bless you, as he promised you, and you shall lend to many nations, but you shall not borrow, and you shall rule over many nations, but they shall not rule over you.").

It also painted God (Jehovah) as jealous and vengeful who requested the Israelites to destroy, kill and exterminate the peoples who inhabited the land of Canaan (Deuteronomy 20: 16–17: "But in the cities of these peoples that the LORD your God is giving you for an inheritance, you shall save alive nothing that breathes, but you shall devote them to complete destruction, the Hittites and the Amorites, the Canaanites and the Perizzites, the Hivites and the Jebusites, as the LORD your God has commanded…").

No mention of an afterlife could be found in the Torah's five books (Pentateuch), and what would be the reward and punishment of the good and evil people, apart from the description of the earthly paradise of Eden, and God's punishment of Adam and Eve after they disobeyed Him and the death which was therefore their destiny. In the Hebrew Bible, Sheol is a place of darkness to which the spirit of all the dead go, both the righteous and the unrighteous, regardless of the acts and deeds made in life, (Genesis 37: 35-36: "All his sons and all his daughters rose up to comfort him, but he refused to be comforted and said, No, I shall go down to Sheol to my son, mourning."), (Psalms 6: 5: "For in death there is no remembrance of you; in Sheol who will give your praise."), (Ecclesiastes 9: 10: "Whatever your hand finds to do, do it with your might, for there is no work or thought or knowledge or wisdom in Sheol, to which you are going.).The Hebrews believed that the spirit of a person is eternal.

Later after the destruction of the first temple and the Babylonian exile (586 BC), the interpretation of Sheol changed for certain Hebrew prophets as we read in Prophet Daniel (12: 2-3: "And many of those who sleep in the dust of the earth shall awake, some to everlasting life, and some to shame and everlasting contempt. And those who are wise shall shine like the brightness of the sky above; and those who turn many to righteousness, like the stars forever and ever.").

With repeated military defeats and episodes of exile and dislocation culminating in the destruction of the Second Temple in AD 70 and the Jewish dispersion from Judea and

Samaria (diaspora), Jewish thinkers began to lose hope in an earthly kingdom and started investing greater expectations in a messianic future.

The Israelites believe in the appearance of a Messiah (a saviour anointed by God) who would deliver the Jewish people from their oppressors, who will establish an eternal earthly kingdom for the people of Israel (Deuteronomy 18: 18–19: "I will raise up for them a prophet like you from among their brothers. And I will put my words in his mouth, and he shall speak to them all that I command him. And whoever will not listen to my words that he shall speak in my name, I myself will require it of him.").

Chapter Three

The Greeks and their religious beliefs – The Greek philosophers

The Greeks are an Indo-European people who lived in the Balkan Peninsula and the territories surrounding the Aegean Sea. Their entry into history begins with the history of the Island of Crete in the second millennia BC, which was in contact with the civilizations of Egypt and the Levantine cities (present day Syria, Lebanon and Palestine). The Greek civilization attained its apogee after the victory of the City of Athens and its allied cities over the Persian Empire during the fifth century BC.

In the period preceding this victory as well as a result of it, prominent figures came to be known worldwide as the statesmen Solon and Pericles, poets and writers Homer and Hesiod, philosophers Thales, Socrates, Plato, Aristotle and later Plotinus, historians Herodotus, Thucydides and Xenophon, artists and theatre writers Sophocles and Euripides, scientists Archimedes, Euclid and Pythagoras, and geographers Ptolemy and Eurathostenes. The Ancient Greeks believed in many gods and goddesses and many other semi-divine figures such as Zeus, Apollo, Poseidon, Aphrodite, Athena, Dionysus, etc... They created images and statues of their deities for many purposes, not unlike the peoples of Mesopotamia and Egypt. The Greek philosophers (in translation: friends of wisdom) goal was mainly the attainment of truth, justice and harmony for society through the study and analysis of relations between members of the society and also the surrounding natural phenomena, using in the process reason and logic in the quest for knowledge. Some of them came to believe in the existence of an invisible and unchanging Supreme Being.

Socrates was born in Athens in 469 BC. His famous student, Plato, called him, "The wisest, most just, and best of all men whom I have ever known".

It was the truth that he loved and believed in. He believed in an Eternal Soul full of all knowledge. He believed that there was a difference between what our senses might tell us and the actual truth. He felt that access to the truth could not be achieved by just studying the external phenomena but by using reason. He taught that there are two worlds: a visible world of ever-changing phenomena and another one invisible and unchanging which controls the visible changing one. He taught that the philosophical mind includes reason, will and desire in balance and harmony. And that wisdom is the knowledge of what is right and the correct relationship between all of what exists. He emphasized the existence of an Absolute Justice in the world.

He suggested that what is considered a good act is not good because gods say it is, but is good because it is useful to us in our efforts to be better and happier people. That ethics are not a matter of following the gods or scriptures for what is good or bad, but rather acting according to reason.

*

Socrates himself never wrote any of his ideas down, possibly to avoid problems with simple-minded people, but rather engaged his students in conversations. Plato reconstructed these discussions in a great set of writings known as The Dialogs. Socrates disagreed with the beliefs of fellow Greeks in the existence of many gods and called for the existence of a

Supreme Eternal Soul who is the origin of all existence and the source of all virtue.

*

Plato born in 437 BC was Socrates' prized student. After Socrates' death, he founded in 386 BC the Academy. As his teacher, Plato divided reality into two: on the one hand an ideal, which is ultimate reality, permanent, eternal, spiritual. On the other hand, the phenomena: things as they seem to us, associated with matter, time, and space. Phenomena are illusions, which decay and die. Ideals are unchanging, perfect.

Ideals are available to us through our thought, while phenomena are available to us through our senses, and he argued that thought is a vastly superior means to get to the truth. Senses can only give us information about the ever-changing and imperfect world of phenomena, and so can only provide implications about ultimate reality, not reality itself. Reason goes straight to the ideal.

According to Plato, the phenomenal world strives to become ideal and perfect. Ideals are, in that sense, a motivating force. In fact, he identifies the ideal with God who is perfect goodness. In his book: *The Republic* (η πολιτεια) Book VI Chapter e we read: "The eyes possessor... will see nothing... of the object... and the colours will remain invisible unless a third element is present: what you call light. The Good has begotten it in its own likeness and it bears the same relation to sight and visible objects... that the Good bears to intelligence and intelligible objects in the intelligible realm".

"What gives the objects of knowledge their truth and the knower's mind the power of knowing is the form of the Good. It is the cause of knowledge and truth... and yet it is even more splendid than knowledge and truth... but it is wrong to think of either as being the Good, whose position is ranked still higher".

God created the world out of matter and shaped it according to his ideal. According to Plato, if the world is not perfect, it is not because of God but because the raw materials were not perfect. In a similar way so are the human beings: the body is material and mortal, and the soul is ideal and immortal. The soul includes reason as well as self-awareness and moral sense. The soul is drawn to the good, the ideal, and so is drawn to God.

Plato talks about three souls. One soul he called appetite, which is mortal and comes from our need for food. The second soul he called spirit or courage and is also mortal, and lives in the heart. The third soul is reason. It is immortal and resides in the brain.

Plato's philosophical ideas about the society covered the search for a fair government and a society based on virtue. His ideas are contained in his book: *The Republic*, where he discusses the education of different classes of society, and especially that of the Guardians (Rulers/Philosophers), but also his books: *The Laws* and *The Statesman*.

In *The Republic*, he divides society into three elements and compares the elements of his society to three souls: The peasants represent the appetite and are the ones who till the soil to produce food, i.e. take care of society's basic appetites. The warriors represent the spirit and courage of the society. And the philosopher king with reason guides the society. Plato includes women as men's equals in his system.

*

Aristotle was born in 384 BC in a small Greek city in Thrace. He joined Plato's Academy about 376 BC until the death of Plato in 347 BC and disagreed with Plato on many points. For four years, Aristotle served as the teacher of thirteen-year-old Alexander, son of Philip of Macedon. In 334 BC, he returned to Athens and established his school of philosophy in a set of buildings called the Lyceum.

Aristotle was as much a scientist as a philosopher. He was fascinated with nature, and went a long way towards classifying the plants and animals of Greece. He was equally interested in studying the anatomies of animals. Besides plants and animals, his studies included the study of solid mater and astronomy. He established the basis of the experimental methodology in science.

His point of disagreement with Plato was that the ideal should be found "inside" the phenomena, the universals "inside" the particulars. What Plato called ideal, Aristotle called essence, and its opposite, he referred to as matter. Essence is what provides the shape, form and purpose to matter. Essence is perfect, complete, but has no substance, no solidity. According to Aristotle, essence and matter need each other.

Like Plato, he postulates three kinds of souls, although slightly differently defined. There is a plant soul, the essence of which is nutrition. Then there is an animal soul, which contains the basic sensations, desire, pain and pleasure, and the ability to cause motion. Last is the human soul. The essence of the human soul is, of course, reason. He suggests that, perhaps, this last soul is capable of existence apart from the body.

*

Plotinus was born about AD 205 and is considered one of the late Ancient Greek philosophers. He made his studies in Alexandria, later travelled to Persia where he got in contact with Persian and Hindu philosophies.

Plotinus taught about the existence of a "ONE" existing eternally representing absolute Perfection and Beauty, who could be defined as the force without which nothing could exist. According to Plotinus, the "ONE" does not work and is not conscientious of Himself. The "ONE" consists of Reason and Mater.

Plotinus compared the "ONE" to light, the reason to the sun and the spirit to the moon, which takes its light from the sun, while the light exists without the need for any celestial body. Similarly, the less perfect creature takes its light from the more perfect, so that all creatures take their light from the "ONE" without the "ONE's" express desire.

It looks as if Plotinus tried to establish a competing philosophy to Christianity, which was fast spreading into the Roman Empire. His philosophy takes many of its components from Plato and Socrates but also from Ancient Persian and Hindu philosophies.

Chapter Four

Ancient Hindu and Persian religions

The Hindu religion

The Hindu religion appeared in about 1500 BC after the Arian (Scythian) migrations to India, whereby their pagan beliefs mixed up gradually with the beliefs and worship of the indigenous peoples of India. It is a synthesis of various Indian cultures and traditions, with diverse roots and no founder.

Prominent themes in Hindu beliefs include: "Dharma" (ethics/duties), "Artha" (prosperity/work), "Kama" (emotions/ sexuality), "Samsara" (the continuing cycle of birth, life, death and rebirth), "Karma" (action, intent and consequences), "Moksha" (liberation from Samsara or liberation in this life), and the various Yoga practices.

"Dharma" is considered an important goal in Hinduism. It includes behaviours that makes life better, and includes duties, rights and good conduct.

"Artha" is virtuous pursuit of wealth for livelihood and economic prosperity. It is inclusive of political life and material well-being. The proper pursuit of "Artha" is considered an important aim of human life in Hinduism.

"Kama" means desire, wish, passion and pleasure of the senses. It is considered an essential and healthy goal of human life when pursued without sacrificing Dharma, Artha and Moksha.

"Moksha" is the ultimate goal of life. It is associated with liberation from sorrow, suffering and "Saṃsara" (birth-rebirth cycle), particularly in polytheistic schools of Hinduism. In other schools, such as the monistic schools, "Moksha" is a goal achievable in current life, as a state of bliss through self-realization, of comprehending the nature of one's soul.

"Karma" is the law of cause and effect for actions that may be ethical or non-ethical, the consequence of these actions and the rebirth. These actions may be those in a person's current life, or, in some schools of Hinduism, actions in their past lives; furthermore, the consequences may result in a person's current life, or future lives.

This cycle of birth, life, death and rebirth is called Samsara.

The Concept of God in Hinduism is diverse spanning monotheism, polytheism, monism, and atheism; and its concept of God is complex and depends upon the philosophy followed by each individual. It sometimes involves devotion to a single god while accepting the existence of others.

The "One Truth" of Vedic literature, in modern era scholarship, has been interpreted as monotheism and monism, as well as deified Hidden Principles behind the great happenings and processes of nature.

Hindus believe that all living creatures have a soul. The soul is believed to be eternal. The goal of life, according to the Advaita School, is to achieve one's soul to be identical to the Supreme Soul (Brahman). The Dvaita and Bhakti schools understand Brahman as a Supreme Being separate from individual souls. They worship the Supreme Being variously as Vishnu, Brahma, Shiva, or Shakti, depending upon the person's sect.

The Yoga school of Hinduism accepts the concept of a "personal god" and left it to the Hindu to define his or her god. Recent estimates place the current number of Hindus at around 1.3 billion, with most living in India.

The Buddhist religion

The Buddhist religion appeared in India about 500 BC and its mythical establisher is Prince Gautama Buddha, commonly known as the Buddha "the awakened one". At the beginning and before it evolved into different sects, it was not a religion in the proper sense of the word, but consisted of philosophical ideas by the Buddha who taught ways to avoid suffering and misery through the elimination of ignorance and craving, in order to reach lasting happiness, which according to him could be attained by training the mind through spiritual practice in order to reach permanent inner peace or "Nirvana".

Within Buddhism "Samsara" is defined as the continual repetitive cycle of birth, life, death and rebirth. "Samsara" arises out of ignorance and is characterized by suffering, anxiety and dissatisfaction. Liberation from "Samsara" is possible by following the Buddhist path in order to achieve permanent inner peace or "Nirvana". Once a person attains "Nirvana" he shall be happy throughout his life, and in life after life.

The doctrine of "Anatta" rejects the concepts of a permanent eternal soul, as it is called in Hinduism, Judaism and Christianity. Rebirth in subsequent existences must not be understood as the reincarnation of one's soul from one existence to the next.

One consistent belief held by all Buddhist schools is the lack of a creator deity. Buddhism encompasses a variety of traditions, beliefs and spiritual practices. Recent estimates place the current number of Buddhists at around 530 million, with most living in South-East Asia.

Zoroastrianism

Zoroastrianism is the old religion of Persia ascribed to the teachings of the prophet Zoroaster (Zardosht in Persian), whose Supreme Being was Ahura Mazda (Wise Lord). It is one of the world's oldest religions. The Zoroastrian name of the religion is Mazdayasna, which combines Mazda (Lord) with the word Yasna (worship).

Ahura Mazda's creation is Asha (truth and order) and is the antithesis of chaos. Chaos is represented by Angra Mainyu (Angry Spirit) also referred to as the Destructive Principle (Ahriman), while the benevolent is represented through Ahura Mazda's Spenta Mainyu (Good Spirit). It is through Spenta Mainyu that Ahura Mazda manifests itself to humankind, and through which the Creator interacts with the world.

It combines dualism and monotheism in a manner unique among the major religions of the world. For a thousand years, forms of Zoroastrianism were serving as the state religion of pre-Islamic Iranian empires from around 600 BC to AD 650. Zoroastrianism was suppressed following the Muslim conquest of Persia. Recent estimates place the current number of Zoroastrians at around 2.7 million, with most living in India and Iran.

Leading characteristics, such as Messianism, the Golden Rule, heaven and hell, and free will influenced other religious systems, including Second Temple Judaism, Gnosticism, Christianity, and Islam. In Zoroastrianism, the purpose in life is to, "be among those who renew the world, to make the world progress towards perfection". Its basic maxims include:

- Good Thoughts, Good Words, Good Deeds.
- There is only one path and that is the path of Truth.
- Do the right thing, and then all beneficial rewards will come to you.

The most important texts of the religion are those of the "Avesta", which includes the writings of Zoroaster known as the Gathas that define the religion's precepts, and the "Yasna", the worship. Zoroaster proclaimed that there is only one God, the singularly creative and sustaining force of the universe. He also stated that human beings are given a right of choice, and because of cause and effect are also responsible for the consequences of their choices. Zoroaster's teachings focused on responsibility. Post-Zoroastrian scripture introduced the concept of Ahriman, the Devil, which was effectively a personification of Angra Mainyu.

Chapter Five

Christianity

5. A. The socio-political situation in Palestine during the Roman Period

After the conquest of Alexander the Great (330 BC), Palestine was ruled at first by the Ptolemy kings of Egypt, a dynasty founded by Ptolemaic 1st Sotir, a general of Alexander and shortly thereafter by the Seleucid kings of Syria, a dynasty founded by Seleucos 1st Nicator, another general of Alexander. Due to the settlement of a considerable number of Macedonians and Greeks in Syria and Egypt, the population of Palestine consisted mostly of Hebrews living in Judea and Samaria, Canaanites, Phoenicians, Arameans, Philistines and Greeks alongside the coast and in Galilee, with Greeks mostly in the main cities.

Before the Roman conquest in 63 BC, and during the rule of the Seleucids dynasty, the Jews rose against the kings of Syria, and under the leadership of the brothers Maccabaeus succeeded to win their independence (from 142 to 67 BC). The Seleucids regained control over Palestine for a short period but were never able to impose their pagan beliefs on the Jewish population of Palestine, although they introduced many aspects of their Hellenic civilization and way of life which included the construction of amphitheatres, gymnasiums, public baths, agoras, etc....

After the Roman conquest of Syria and Palestine, and due to the existence of many Greeks living in Syria and Palestine and also the admiration the Romans held towards the Greek civilization and its closeness to their own way of life, the Hellenistic (a mixture of Greek, and Levantine culture) culture continued its existence under the Romans in Asia Minor, Syria, and Palestine, and the Greek language continued being used and was the language of the educated society while the Latin language use was limited to the army and justice.

From the above described, we can understand the desire of the Jewish people for emancipation from the rule of the new Roman conqueror. The Jews detested Rome as the latest of a long line of conquerors, partly because of its imposition of taxes, which had to be paid to the foreigner. They were also bitterly divided between themselves: The Pharisees, who believed in the resurrection of the dead and a divine Last Judgement, were fighting against the Sadducees, and the zealots were organizing a nationalist resistance against the foreigner and waiting for the advent of the promised in the Torah Messiah, who will liberate them from this foreign pagan rule, allowing them to re-establish their kingdom over the Land of Israel which shall extend from the Nile to the Euphrates and be ruled according to the Torah laws.

Jesus of Nazareth was born during this period of Roman occupation.

5. B. The life of Jesus and his teaching

Jesus (Isa of the Koran) was born in about 6 BC in the small town of Bethlehem (Bread house in Aramean) of Judea during the rule of Roman Emperor Augustus Caesar. He grew up in the town of Nazareth from which he took his name: The Nazarene. The four evangels – gospels (the word evangel means happy news in Greek) according to Matthew, Mark, Luke, and John, which were acknowledged as canonical by the Christian Churches in the fourth century AD, give us a glimpse of the life and teachings of Jesus, his mission to save the human race from the sin of Adam the first man, who was expelled by God from the Garden of Eden and punished with death and a life of suffering due to his disobedience.

The evangels teach us about:

- The miraculous birth of Jesus as in (Matthew 1: 18–21: "When his mother Mary had been betrothed to Joseph, before they came together she was found to be with child of the Holy Spirit; and her husband Joseph, being a just man and unwilling to put her to shame, resolved to divorce her quietly. But as he considered this, an angel of the Lord appeared to him in a dream, saying, Joseph, son of David, do not fear to take Mary your wife, for that which is conceived in her is of the Holy Spirit; she will bear a son, and you shall call his name Jesus, for he will save his people from their sins."), also in (Luke 1: 26–35).
- We find the same account in the Koran (Surah 3: 45–47), (Surah 4: 171), as Mary conceived from the Holy Spirit (the Holy Spirit of God) and gave birth to Jesus, God having chosen her from between all women and purified her from sin (Matthew 1: 18–22), (Luke 1: 26–35) but also in the Koran (Surah 3: 42).

- He didn't have a human father as all the other creatures as accounted for also in the Koran (Surah 4: 171: "The Messiah, Jesus son of Mary, was only a messenger of Allah, and His Word which He conveyed unto Mary, and a Spirit from Him…"). We find Jesus called "Jesus son of Mary" in all the surahs of the Koran, probably to confirm that Jesus didn't had a human father, as he would have been called in patriarchal Arabia if Jesus had one, but only a human mother.

- The miracles that Jesus made, which included the healing of the sick and the resurrection of the dead (Matthew 15: 28–30, 32–38), (Mark 1: 32–34) and (Mark 5: 35–42), but also in the Koran (Surah 3: 49: "… I fashion for you out of clay the likeness of a bird, and I breathe into it and it is a bird, by Allah's leave. I heal him who was born blind, and the leper, and I raise the dead, by Allah's leave…"). The same text also reported in (Surah 5: 110).

- Jesus's teachings are based on love and the tolerance of the other.

  The love and forgiveness requested by Jesus are expressed in (Matthew 7: 12: "So whatever you wish that men would do to you, do so to them; for this is the Law and the prophets."), (Matthew 5: 38–41: "You have heard that it was said, 'An eye for an eye and a tooth for a tooth'. But I say to you, do not resist one who is evil. But if any one strikes you on the right cheek, turn to him the other also; and if anyone would sue you and take your coat, let him have your cloak as well; and if any one forces you to go one mile, go with him two miles").

  Also in (Matthew 5: 44–48: "But I say to you, Love your enemies and pray for those who persecute you, so that you may be sons of your Father who is in heaven; for he makes his sun rise on the evil and on the good, and sends rain on the just and on the unjust. For if you love those who love you, what reward have you? Do not even the tax collectors do the same? And if you salute only your brethren, what more are you doing than others? Do not even the Gentiles do the same? You, therefore, must be perfect, as your Heavenly Father is perfect").

The Jewish Rabbis were surprised by his teaching as it was against Moses' Law (Levites 24: 19–20: "Anyone who inflicts a permanent injury on his or her neighbour shall receive the same in return: fracture for fracture, eye for eye, tooth for tooth. The same injury that one gives another shall be inflicted in return."). But the tolerance and forgiveness Jesus taught had its limits as expressed in (Matthew 7: 6: "Do not give dogs what is holy; and do not throw your pearls before swine, lest they trample them under foot and turn to attack you."), so that His request for forgiveness shall not go beyond a certain limit: that of defending a person's own life.

- In self-criticism, we provide the following excerpt from (Matthew 7: 3–5: "Why do you see the speck that is in your brother's eye, but do not notice the log that is in your own eye? Or how can you say to your brother: Let me take the speck out of your eye, when there is the log in your own eye? You hypocrite, first take the log out of your own eye, and then you will see clearly to take the speck out of your brother's eye."), so that self-criticism of a person's deeds is required in order to achieve self-control and not repeat one's mistakes.
- In humility, Jesus gave the good example by washing the feet of his disciples as per (John 13: 12–15: "So when he had washed their feet... he said to them, Do you realize what I have done for you? You call me 'teacher' and 'master,' and rightly so, for indeed I am. If I, therefore, the master and teacher, have washed your feet, you ought to wash one another's feet. I have

given you a model to follow, so that as I have done for you, you should also do"). And in (Luke 22: 25–26: "He said to them: The kings of the Gentiles lord it over them and those in authority over them are addressed as 'Benefactors'; but among you it shall not be so. Rather, let the greatest among you be as the youngest, and the leader as the servant").

How that would have been beneficial if carried out by our present leaders and statesmen!

- In charity and assistance to the poor, Jesus requested assisting the poor and sharing one's possessions with the needy persons as per (Matthew 19: 21: "If you want to be perfect, go, sell what you possess and give to the poor, and you will have treasure in heaven"…), and when practicing charity, how to carry it out as in (Matthew 6: 1–4: "Beware of practicing your piety before men in order to be seen by them; for then you will have no reward from your Father who is in heaven. Thus, when you give alms, sound no trumpet before you, as the hypocrites do in the synagogues and in the streets, that they may be praised by men. Truly, I say to you, they have received their reward. But when you give alms, do not let your left hand know what your right hand is doing, so that your alms may be in secret; and your Father who sees in secret will reward you").

- In defining what's pure and impure food for consumption Jesus taught his disciples that not what is eaten makes a person bad, but what comes out of the heart and mouth as in (Matthew 15: 10–20: "… not what goes into the mouth defiles a man, but what comes out of the mouth, this defiles a man… Do you not see that whatever goes into the mouth passes into the stomach, and so passes on? But what comes out of the mouth proceeds from the heart, and this defiles a man. For out of the heart come evil thoughts, murder, adultery, fornication, theft, false witness, slander. These are what defile a man").

- About the manner prayer should be addressed to God, Jesus taught in (Matthew 6: 5–15: "And when you pray, you must not be like the hypocrites; for they love to stand and pray in the synagogues and at the street corners, that they may be seen by men. Truly, I say to you, they have received their reward". But when you pray, go into your room and shut the door and pray to your Father who is in secret; and your Father who sees in secret will reward you. And in praying do not heap up empty phrases as the Gentiles do; for they think that they will be heard for their many words. Do not be like them, for your Father knows what you need before you ask him."

- Pray, then, like this:
  "Our Father who art in heaven, Hallowed be thy name. May your kingdom come. May your will be done, on earth as it is in heaven. Give us this day our daily bread and forgive us our trespasses, as we forgive those who trespass against us; and lead us not into temptation, but deliver us from evil".

- "For if you forgive men their trespasses, your heavenly Father also will forgive you; but if you do not forgive men their trespasses, neither will your Father forgive your trespasses.").

- In answer to the Pharisees who asked him if it is allowed to pay the tribute to Caesar he answered (Mark 12: 14-17: "… they say unto him… Is it lawful to give tribute unto Caesar, or not? Shall we give, or shall we not give? But he, knowing their hypocrisy, said unto them:…. bring me a denarius, that I may see it. And they brought it. And he saith unto them, Whose is this image and superscription? And they said unto him, Caesar's. And Jesus said unto them, Render unto Caesar the things that are Caesar's, and unto God the things that are God's...."). Thus He separated the religious and spiritual from man-made laws.

- Showing God's love to humankind, Jesus told the people in (Matthew 6: 25–30: "Therefore I tell you, do not be anxious about your life, what you shall eat or what you shall drink, nor about your body, what you shall put on... Look at the birds of the air: they neither sow nor reap nor gather into barns, and yet your heavenly Father feeds them. Are you not of more value than they? And which of you by being anxious can add one cubit to his span of life? And why are you anxious about clothing? Consider the lilies of the field, how they grow; they neither toil nor spin; yet I tell you, even Solomon in all his glory was not arrayed like one of these. But if God so clothes the grass of the field, which today is alive and tomorrow is thrown into the oven, will he not much more clothe you, O men of little faith?").

- Exposing God's Justice, Goodness and Mercy for humankind, taking into account the suffering that some had to endure not due to a fault of their own making, but due to wars, natural disasters, and persecution by others, Jesus proclaimed: (Matthew 5:
3: "Blessed are they who hunger for the Spirit, for theirs is the kingdom of heaven.
4: Blessed are they who mourn, for they shall be comforted.
5: Blessed are the meek, for they shall inherit the land.
6: Blessed are they who hunger and thirst for righteousness, for they will be satisfied.
7: Blessed are the merciful, for they shall obtain mercy.
8: Blessed are the clean of heart, for they will see God.

9: Blessed are the peacemakers, for they will be called children of God.
10 Blessed are they who are persecuted for the sake of righteousness, for theirs is the kingdom of heaven."

The above was part of the Sermon on the Mount (Matthew 5), one of the most important speeches of Jesus.

But contrary to Evangelist Matthew (Matthew 5: 17) and many other contemporaries beliefs that the New Testament complemented the Old Testament, Jesus teaching is in fact a complete abrogation of the Old Testament for the following reasons:

1. The God of the New Testament is a loving God to all human kind in contrast to the vengeful and jealous tribal God (Jehovah) of the Old Testament who requested the destruction and killing of peoples living in the land of Canaan, including women and children (Deuteronomy 20: 16–17: "However, in the cities of the nations the Lord your God is giving you as an inheritance, do not leave alive anything that breathes. Completely destroy them: the Hittites, Amorites, Canaanites, Perizzites, Hivites and Jebusites – as the Lord your God has commanded you.").

2. The Messiah of the New Testament is not an earthly ruler as the one referred to in the Old Testament and as King David or Solomon, but a ruler of a heavenly eternal kingdom, who will come at the end of the age to judge the living and the dead, being given that authority by God.

3. The New Testament is not destined only for the Children of Israel, but for the whole humanity as per (Matthew 28: 18–20: "… All authority in heaven and on earth has been given to me. Go therefore and make disciples of all nations, baptizing them in the name of

the Father and of the Son and of the Holy Spirit... and lo, I am with you always, to the close of the age.").

4. The Law of Moses in its minutia with all it contains in ways of worship, sacrifices, purifications, eating, drinking and clothing are not any more required for one's soul saving. As already mentioned above, Jesus abolished the held beliefs about food impurity (Matthew 15: 10–20). Regarding the rules of men's behaviour, he summarized them in (Matthew 7: 12: "So whatever you wish that men would do to you, do so to them; for this is the Law and the prophets.") and he requested his followers to abide by men's established laws, as long as they do not contradict the ethics as mentioned in (Mark 12: 14–17).

And Jesus denounced the practices of the Jewish Rabbis – teachers of Moses' Law, as per his admonition to some of them as in (Luke 11: 46–52: "And he said, Woe also to you scholars of the Law! You impose on people burdens hard to carry, but you yourselves do not lift one finger to touch them..... Woe to you, scholars of the Law! You have taken away the key of knowledge. You yourselves did not enter and you stopped those trying to enter."). He invited people not to stick to the exact wording of Moses' Law but to its spirit. He concentrated in his teaching on people's ethical behaviour and taught that all men are brothers in humanity. The essence of His teaching consisted in good and fair treatment of one's neighbour and that the achievement of perfection lies in loving one's neighbour as much as oneself.

It is here important to mention apostle Paul's interpretation of Jesus teaching related to Moses' Law as in his epistle to the Church of Rome (Chapter 2: 14-16: "For when the Gentiles who do not have the Law, by nature observe the prescriptions of the Law, they are a law for themselves even though they do not have the Law. They show that the demands of the Law are written in their hearts, while their conscience also bears witness and their conflicting thoughts accuse or even defend them on the day when, according to my gospel, God will judge people's hidden works through Christ Jesus.), also in (Chapter 2: 28–29: "One is not a Jew outwardly. True circumcision is not outward, in the flesh. Rather, one is a Jew inwardly, and circumcision is of the heart, in the spirit, not the letter; his praise is not from human beings but from God."). Apostle Paul here explains that the ground for our justification before God is our faith in the Lord Jesus Christ and the observance of his teaching and good deeds as distinguished from the observance of Moses' Law's rules. He was led to this discussion by the teaching of certain Jews that we are to be justified by keeping the Law to the letter. To the defence of his doctrine and the refutation of objections to it, the apostle devotes the first eleven chapters of his Epistle to the Church of Rome.

5. Jesus abolished the sanctity of the Sabbath (Mark 2: 24-27: "And the Pharisees said unto him, Behold, why do they on the Sabbath day that which is not lawful? ... And he said unto them: The Sabbath was made for man, and not man for the Sabbath: so that the Son of Man is lord even of the Sabbath."). The Son of Man here is Jesus Christ.

6. Christ the Saviour: Jesus told his disciples about his death and resurrection on many occasions, the last one at the last super, before being handed over to the Jewish tribunal (Matthew 26: 26–29: "Now as they were eating, Jesus took bread, and when he had said the blessing he broke it and gave it to the disciples. 'Take it and eat,' he said, 'this is my body'. Then he

took a cup, and when he had given thanks he handed it to them saying, 'Drink from this, all of you, for this is my blood, the blood of the covenant, poured out for many for the forgiveness of sins. From now on, I tell you, I shall never again drink wine until the day I drink the new wine with you in the kingdom of my Father'."). The priest during communion, when sharing bread and wine with the believers, reminds them of Jesus sacrifice of his life to save humanity of the original sin of Adam, opening for them again the gates of eternal life, conditional on true repentance.

The death and resurrection of Christ (Al-Massih in Arabic) is mentioned in the Koran as well (Surah 3: 55: "when Allah said: O Jesus! I am allowing your death and causing you to ascend unto Me, and I am cleansing you of those who disbelieve and setting those who follow you above those who disbelieve until the Day of Resurrection....").

So, Jesus Christ who was delivered to the Roman Governor to be persecuted and crucified was resurrected by God in body and soul from death and ascended to God according to eyewitnesses (Matthew 27: 57–66: "When it was evening, there came a rich man from Arimathea named Joseph, who was himself a disciple of Jesus. He went to Pilate and asked for the body of Jesus; then Pilate ordered it to be handed over. So Joseph took the body, wrapped it in a clean shroud and put it in his own new tomb, which he had hewn out of the rock. He then rolled a large stone across the entrance of the tomb and went away.... Next day... the chief priests and the Pharisees went and made the sepulchre secure, putting seals on the stone and mounting a guard...."), (Matthew 28: 1–6: "After the Sabbath, as the first day of the week was dawning, Mary Magdalene and the other Mary came to see the tomb. And behold, there was a great earthquake, for an angel of the Lord descended from heaven, approached, rolled back the stone, and sat upon it. His appearance was like lightning and his clothing was white as snow. The guards were shaken with fear of him and became like dead men. Then the angel said to the women in reply: Do not be afraid! I know that you are seeking Jesus the crucified. He is not here, for he has been raised just as he said. Come and see the place where he lay").

According to the Evangels, He is the only human being in God's presence until the Day of Resurrection. He is the saviour of the human race, sent by God to deliver it from the original sin of the first man Adam, who committed sin and was banned from Paradise. For Christians, He is the New Adam.

7. Punishment and reward in the afterlife:

No detailed description of Paradise and Hell exists in the New Testament, comparable to what we find in the Koran, the only mention being that about the Last Judgment as in (Matthew 25: 31–46: "When the Son of Man comes in his glory, and all the angels with him... Before him will be gathered all the nations, and he will separate them one from another as a shepherd separates the sheep from the goats, and he will place the sheep at his right hand, but the goats at the left. Then, the King will say to those at his right hand, 'Come, O blessed of my Father, inherit the kingdom prepared for you from the foundation of the world; for I was hungry and you gave me food, I was thirsty and you gave me drink, I was a stranger and you welcomed me, I was naked and you clothed me, I was sick and you visited me, I was in prison and you came to me.' Then the righteous will answer him, 'Lord, when did we see thee hungry and feed thee, or thirsty...' And the

King will answer them, 'Truly, I say to you, as you did it to one of the least of these my brethren, you did it to me.' Then he will say to those at his left hand, 'Depart from me, you cursed, into the eternal fire prepared for the devil and his angels; for I was hungry and you gave me no food, I was thirsty and you gave me no drink,... And they will go away into eternal punishment, but the righteous into eternal life").

Also, a mention of the suffering in hell is described in the tale of the Rich and the Poor in (Luke 16: 19–26: "There was a rich man who dressed in purple garments and fine linen and dined sumptuously each day. Lying at his door was a poor man named Lazarus, covered with sores, who would gladly have eaten his fill of the scraps that fell from the rich man's table. Dogs even used to come and lick his sores. When the poor man died, he was carried away by angels to the bosom of Abraham. The rich man also died and was buried and from the netherworld, where he was in torment, he raised his eyes and saw Abraham far off and Lazarus at his side. He cried out, 'Father Abraham, have pity on me. Send Lazarus to dip the tip of his finger in water and cool my tongue, for I am suffering torment in these flames'. Abraham replied, 'My child, remember that you received what was good during your lifetime while Lazarus likewise received what was bad; but now he is comforted here, whereas you are tormented. Moreover, between us and you a great chasm is established to prevent anyone from crossing who might wish to go from our side to yours or from your side to ours'.").

*

Most Christians believe in the resurrection of the body and the soul, and believe that Jesus Christ, the Son of Man, and God's

Word who didn't commit a single sin in his life, who suffered and sacrificed his life and died on the cross due to his love for human kind was resurrected from death by God and is the New Adam who reopened the gates of eternal life to human kind. And that the Merciful God sent him to human kind as a demonstration of His love.

In what concerns Moses' Law, the Christians believe that it consists essentially of the Ten Commandments of God, given to Moses on Mount Sinai, which they have to observe, and do not feel obliged to stick to the exact wording of the other requirements of Moses' Law, but only to its spirit, as these were abrogated by Jesus.

5. C. The canonical evangels and their writers

All four canonical evangels were written during the first century AD and according to many historians, the first evangel was written by:

- Matthew, one of Jesus twelve disciples, around AD 55 in Aramaic (Syriac) using the Hebrew alphabet, for Jewish converts to Christianity in Palestine and Syria. Some sources wrote that the Apostle Matthew travelled to Syria and might have gone to the roman province of Arabia to preach the evangel.

  Matthew's evangel is directed to an audience steeped in Hebrew tradition. The evangel of Matthew stressed that Jesus is the Messiah (1:16, 16:16) or Christ foretold in the Old Testament, and that the Kingdom of the Lord Jesus is the Kingdom of Heaven.

  The Evangel of Matthew is one of the most quoted books of the Bible. Noted especially for "Jesus' Sermon on the Mount" in Chapters 5–7, Matthew is the source of the Beatitudes (5: 1–10) and the Lord's Prayer (6: 9–13). According to the USCCB Mission (US Conference of Catholic Bishops), the position of the Gospel of Matthew as the first of the four gospels in the New Testament reflects both the view that it was the first to be written, a view that goes back to the late second century AD, and the esteem in which it was held by the church; no other was so frequently quoted in the non-canonical literature of earliest Christianity.

  The Christian philosopher Origen who lived in Egypt around AD 185–254 stated that, "among the four gospels, Matthew, the one-time tax collector who later became a disciple of Jesus, first composed the gospel for the converts from Judaism, published in the Hebrew language" (*Eusebius, Historia Ecclesiastica,*

6.25). This coincides with St Jerome's assessment, in which he stated, "Matthew, also called Levi, apostle and previously publican, composed a gospel of Christ at first published in Judea in Hebrew for the sake of those of the circumcision who believed, but this was afterwards translated into Greek, though by what author is uncertain." (*Jerome, Lives of Illustrious Men*, Chapter 3).

- The evangel of Mark was written according to many historians around AD 60-65 during Nero's persecution of the Christians in Rome or the Jewish revolt, as suggested by internal references to war in Judea and to the Jewish persecution. He wrote it in the Greek language. Mark was not a disciple of Jesus but a relative of the apostle Barnabas and accompanied Barnabas and the apostle Paul from Antioch to Cyprus in their missionary journey. He later travelled with Apostle Peter to Rome and was his interpreter. According to the earliest sources, Mark wrote down an eyewitness account of Peter, Jesus' closest disciple. After Peter and Paul's martyrdom in Rome, he returned to Alexandria where he founded the Egyptian Church. He died a martyr in Alexandria in AD 68.

- The evangel of Luke was written in Greek around AD 80. Luke was not a disciple of Jesus but according to Church tradition he was Luke the Evangelist, the companion of Paul in three of the letters attributed to Paul himself. He was an educated man associated with the early Christians in Antioch, Syria. He is the author of the Acts of the Apostles as well. Original copies of the evangel of Luke have not been preserved; the texts available to us today are from the 4th century *Codex Sinaiticus of Alexandria*.

Luke alone from the other three evangelists wrote about the angel's annunciation to Zachariah related to the birth of John the Baptist, but also about Jesus birth.

The main theme of Luke in the Acts of the Apostles theology is the salvation history of human kind by God through Jesus Christ.

• The evangel of John according to many historians was written in Greek in Ephesus in Western Asia Minor around AD 100. His Gospel was written in poetical style and presents a very different picture of Jesus and his ministry from the three other synoptic gospels of Matthew, Mark and Luke, called synoptic because they share many similarities between them.

He alone of the four evangelists started by stating: (John 1: 1: "In the beginning was the Word, and the Word was with God, and the Word was God"), the Word being Jesus Christ, and other assertions, most of these were the subjective opinion of the writer and not the words of Jesus. Jesus in fact kept repeatedly calling himself Son of Man in John's evangel (John 6: 27 & 53, John 8: 28, John 9: 35, etc.) and John contradicts himself further as in (John 14: 28: "for the Father is greater than I", or John 20: 17: "...I am ascending to my Father and your Father, to my God and your God.").

At most, when Jesus asked his disciples as in (Matthew 16: 15–16: "He said to them, But who do you say that I am? Simon Peter replied, "You are the Christ, the Son of the living God."), the same answer he got in Mark 8: 29–30. And when later after being brought to Caiaphas the high Jewish priest and being questioned as to who he is he answered (Matthew 26: 63–64: "... And the high priest said to him: I adjure you by the living God; tell us if you are the Christ, the Son of God. Jesus said to him: You have said so. But I tell you, hereafter you will see *the Son of Man* seated at the right hand of Power, and coming on the clouds of heaven."). We find the same answer in Mark 14: 61-62.

John the writer of the evangel most probably was not a disciple of Jesus, as some pretend. John the disciple of Christ was a simple Hebrew fisherman (Matthew 4: 21), the son of Zebedee and Salome (two Hebrew names) and shouldn't have known good Greek to write his evangel in Greek poetical style, and he would have been close to 90–100 years old when that evangel was written. Most probably, the evangelist John was a Greek who based his evangel on eye witness narrations of certain disciples of Christ. Some historians relate that the bishops of Asia Minor supposedly requested John the evangelist to write his evangel to deal with the heresy of the Ebionites, who asserted that Christ did not exist before his birth from Mary and his baptism. Other scholars are of the opinion that the Evangel of John was composed in two or three stages. Some modern scholars have raised the possibility that John the Apostle, John the Evangelist, and John of Patmos were three separate individuals. In Greek mythology, the gods married humans and their offspring's were also gods, similar to the pharaoh of ancient Egypt who was worshipped as god, and was thought to be son of gods. Roman emperors before Constantine requested their subjects to worship them as gods. The main Christological dispute in fact started later in Alexandria, Egypt (where a Greek Macedonian dynasty established itself as the new pharaohs of Egypt), between Bishop Alexander and the priest Arius, with Alexander adamantly upholding the idea that Christ being son of God is accordingly a true God, basing his view on the evangel of John. It is mostly due to John's evangel that most Christological disputes (Arianism, Nestorianism, Monophysitism, etc.) arose in the Early Christian Church.

The Early Christians were mostly Jews, as Jesus disciples were. The prayer Jesus taught them was to be directed to "Our Father in Heaven", (Mathew 6: 9–13) and not to Jesus, and on the cross dying, he cried: (Matthew 27: 46: "And about three o'clock Jesus cried out in a loud voice: *Eli, Eli, lema sabachthani?* This translates into: *my God, my God, why have you forsaken me?*"). After the adoption of the Nicene Creed, with the Trinity statement, and the assertion that God the Father, God the Son and the Holy Spirit were Gods, the conversion of Jews to the Christian faith stopped. In Judaism, The Messiah (Christ) is not another God, as God is one. The disciples of Jesus would not have followed him if he told them that he is God. He in fact never told them that, as per the evangels of Mathew, Mark and Luke. At most he answered affirmatively when asked by the Chief Priest if he is the Messiah Son of God (Matthew 26: 63–64).

Another subject for discussion is the belief by some that the Bible is literally inspired word for word by God. In fact, historically, the Jewish religious institutions and some Fathers of the Church believed that the Torah, Old and New Testaments were inspired literally by God, but that cannot stand against the fact that God's inspiration which was an idea, used the reasoning and language expression capabilities of a human imperfect person as a tool. Also, when the scriptures were written, the art of writing and copying was not as developed as it is today. The number of people who could read and write was very limited and the scriptures were written after the death of Moses, resurrection of Jesus and the death of Muhammad by many years (tens and hundreds of years). Semitic languages were the first in history to be written with alphabetical letters, but the techniques used to write them were still primitive. For example the Aramaic, Hebrew and Arabic alphabets didn't include vowels, nor at that stage even the Koran which was written in Arabic in the seventh century AD did include vowels and articulations (points and accents), these were added only much later. Copying the scriptures was done by hand as the art of printing was not yet invented, and by hand copying these scriptures during centuries by a multitude of scribes, many mistakes must have occurred. Mistakes also could have occurred while translating from one language to another. I am not mentioning here that some scribes might have added or deleted certain words (or in fact complete sentences) according to their beliefs and/or interpretation. All these facts should lead us to use Reason given to us by God to try to reach the truth. It seems logical to discard as false any texts in the Torah, Old, New Testament and the Koran referring to God's orders to kill and or discriminate between people because of their race, ethnicity and religious beliefs, as well as any ordering the persecution of people in His name, as God who is all Goodness cannot be the initiator of such commands.

As an example of mistakes in translation, in the Aramean and Hebrew languages, God is always called God, and Jesus Christ called Lord (Rabb in Aramean). Some translations might have mistaken the word "lord" for God, which is incorrect. As examples of correct English translations I provide Apostle Paul's epistle to the Church of Rome (Chapter 1: 7: "To all in Rome who are loved by God and called to be his holy people: *Grace and peace to you from God our Father and from the Lord Jesus Christ*"), also in (Chapter 5: 15: "... *For if through the offence of one many be dead, much more the grace of God, and the gift by grace, which is by one man, Jesus Christ, hath abounded unto many*"). Also in Apostle Peter's speech to the crowds in Acts (Chapter 2: 22-24: "Men of Israel, listen to what I am going to say: *Jesus the Nazarene was a man commended to you by God* by the miracles and portents and signs that God worked through him when he was among you, as you know. *This man*, who was put into your power by the deliberate intention and foreknowledge of God, *you took and had crucified and killed* by men outside the Law. **But God raised him to life**, freeing him from the pangs of Hades…"), also in (Chapter 2: 36: "For this reason the whole House of Israel can be certain **that the Lord and Christ whom God has made is this Jesus whom you crucified**"). In all these texts, the word "Lord" refers to Jesus and not to God who is always called God. There are also other words, which were translated incorrectly without respect to the precise meaning.

At present, due to the developments in sciences, our interpretation of certain scriptures could be different from the interpretation of the fathers of the Church and the Ulema of Islam. For example the age of planet Earth is at present estimated to be about 4.5 billion years and that of the universe more than 14 billion years, that life in its most primitive forms on planet Earth started about one billion years ago, and developed until the present time in accordance with nature's evolutionary laws. Our present-day knowledge does not contradict the scriptures (the Bible and the Koran), where we read that the creation of the universe happened in six days, as these six days are not in fact planet Earth days, but Godly days, and his days could last billions of planet Earth days. The same applies to the Evolution Law, whereby the creation of the first Adam probably took place after primitive forms of life evolved to Homo-Sapiens. **God who created all the physical laws of nature was also the creator of the Evolution Law.**

Most Christian churches today accept that the Bible was not revealed literally word for word by God, although it is of divine inspiration. Hopefully one day, the Muslim religious authorities would accept the same principle regarding the Koran.

5. D. The Acts of the Apostles and their Epistles

The Acts of the Apostles written by the evangelist Luke are based on his close contacts with the disciples of Jesus in Jerusalem, Antioch and Rome (he was the companion of Paul in three of the letters attributed to Paul himself). The Acts complement his evangel and together constitute the theology of the salvation of human kind by God through the life, death and resurrection of Jesus of Nazareth, the promised Messiah. The Acts continue the story of Christianity in the first century, beginning with Jesus' Ascension to Heaven. It describes how the disciples spread the "Good News" in Palestine, Syria and many parts of the Roman Empire, immediately after the resurrection of Jesus, and the difficulties and persecutions they had to endure.

Luke starts his Acts by describing the appearance of Jesus to his disciples in Jerusalem during the forty days after his death and resurrection, his ascension to heaven on the fortieth day and the Day of Pentecost (the coming of the Holy Spirit in the form of incandescent flames on each disciple), fifty days after his ascension to heaven, and the growth of the church in Jerusalem. He quoted Apostle Peter's speech to the Jews in Jerusalem explaining that God sent them the Messiah Jesus for the salvation of humankind from the original sin through his suffering and death, and that God resurrected him from the dead and is therefore the first man in heaven's kingdom. He reported the speech of Apostles Peter and John to the crowds in the Temple and how the head of the Temple guards, the priests and Sadducees jailed and thereafter released them on a promise that they would not address the crowds again and preach about Jesus' mission. How they returned to preach, were jailed again and flogged, the speech of Stephen and his martyrdom.

He described how the early Christians helped each other and shared all what they owned between themselves according to the needs of each of them

Also, he described the conversion of Saul, a Pharisee from the tribe of Benjamin from Tarsus and a Hellenized Jew who witnessed the lynching of Stephen, and persecuted the Christians in Jerusalem. How he was blinded by a heavenly light while he was on his way to Damascus to oppress its Christians, and heard a voice calling him: "Saul, Saul, why are you persecuting me!" When Saul asked what to do, Jesus told him to proceed to Damascus and there he will be shown what is requested of him (Acts: 9, 3–19). Also how the disciple Ananias in Damascus was directed in a dream to meet him.

After Ananias healed his blindness, and spending a certain time in Damascus and the surrounding countryside with Jesus' followers, he became the most fervent follower of Christ. Starting from about AD 47, he began a series of missionary travels which took him from Antioch to Cyprus and Asia Minor, and later all over the eastern part of the Roman Empire, preaching the happy news to the gentiles. His special targets were Jewish proselytes, and gentiles to whom he could preach in Greek. In AD 49 a synod held in Jerusalem at the request of Paul and Barnabas, headed by Apostle Peter, Jacob and John agreed that gentiles would not be required to undergo circumcision to be admitted to the Christian faith. The Christians after his conversion gave him the surname Paul.

Also he describes the apostolic work of Apostle Peter in Lid, Jaffa and Caesarea of Palestine, and the escape of many Christians from Jerusalem, after the martyrdom of Stephan, to Antioch of Syria, Phoenicia and Cyprus.

Apostle Paul wrote many letters to the Christians in Asia Minor, Greece and Rome. These letters have a huge historical importance as they are the earliest Christian documents exposing the beliefs of the early Christians and preceding most of the later written evangels (apart possibly from the evangel of Matthew). In his first letter to the Church of Rome, he confirmed that the mission of Jesus Christ was for all humanity and not only for the Jewish people, who will come one day to believe in him. He exposed the position of the Christian faith regarding Moses' Law and he clarified that following the Law is no longer a prerequisite for redemption from sin, but redemption from sin comes with the belief in Jesus Christ and by following his teaching. In his letter to the church of Galatia 5: 14 he wrote: "*all the Law is condensed in a single command of Jesus: love your neighbour as much as yourselves*". Salvation cannot be acquired by circumcision as per Moses' Law and not by applying Moses' Law's commands literally. Apostle Paul explains at the end of his epistle how Christians should live in accordance with Christian beliefs, as also per his letter to the Christians in Galatia 5: 22–23: "the fruits of the Holy Spirit are love, joy, peace, patience, gentleness, goodness, fidelity and chastity. No law prohibits these things". Also, the duty of the Christians towards each other as per his letter to the people in Galatia 6: 1–4: "Brothers, in case a person is caught in any misconduct, you spiritual persons should set him straight in a humble spirit, looking at yourself, so that you may not be tempted as well. Carry one another's burden and thus fulfil the law of Christ… and let each of you be accountable for his deeds".

5. E. The Apostles Creed (Testimony)

In addition to the four canonical evangels recognized by Christian Churches, The Acts of the Apostles and the Epistles to the Churches in Asia Minor, Greece and Rome, there is the "Apostles' Creed", which is a condensed text of the Early Christians beliefs put together and agreed upon by Jesus disciples, based on Jesus teaching, and inspired by the Holy Spirit.

The first mention of the "Apostles' Creed" occurs in a letter of Saint Ambrose AD 390 from a synod in Milan, and may have been associated with the belief in the fourth century that, under the inspiration of the Holy Spirit, the Twelve Apostles contributed in writing the creed.

It was based on the 2nd-century Rules of Faith and the interrogatory declaration of faith for those receiving Baptism. The English version of the Latin text reads as follows:

"I believe in God the Father almighty, and in Christ Jesus His only Son, our Lord, Who was born from the Holy Spirit and the Virgin Mary, Who under Pontius Pilate was crucified and buried, on the third day rose again from the dead, ascended to heaven, sits at the right hand of the Father, whence He will come to judge the living and the dead, and in the Holy Spirit, the holy Church, the remission of sins, the resurrection of the flesh, the life everlasting.".

The Greek text of Marcellus of Ancyra:

"Πιστεύω οὖν εἰς θεὸν πατέρα παντοκράτορα, καὶ εἰς Χριστὸν Ἰησοῦν, τὸν υἱὸν αὐτοῦ τὸν μονογενῆ, τὸν κύριον ἡμῶν, τὸν γεννηθέντα ἐκ πνεύματος ἁγίου καὶ Μαρίας τῆς παρθένου, τὸν ἐπὶ Ποντίου Πιλάτου σταυρωθέντα καὶ ταφέντα καὶ τῇ τρίτῃ ἡμέρα

ἀναστάντα ἐκ τῶν νεκρῶν, ἀναβάντα εἰς τοὺς
οὐρανούς καὶ καθήμενον ἐν δεξιᾳ τοῦ πατρός, ὅθεν
ἔρχεται κρίνειν ζῶντας καὶ νεκρούς, καὶ εἰς τὸ ἅγιον
πνεῦμα, ἁγίαν ἐκκλησίαν, ἄφεσιν ἁμαρτιῶν, σαρκὸς
ἀνάστασιν, ζωὴν αἰώνιον.".

The two texts Latin and Greek are identical. Later we find the Catholic Church using the following text of the Apostles' Creed:

I believe in God, the Father Almighty, *Creator of heaven and earth*; and in Jesus Christ, His only Son, our Lord: Who was conceived by the Holy Spirit, born of the Virgin Mary; suffered under Pontius Pilate, was crucified, died and was buried. *He descended into hell*; the third day He rose again from the dead; He ascended into heaven, is seated at the right hand of God the Father Almighty; from thence He shall come to judge the living and the dead. I believe in the Holy Spirit, the Holy *Catholic* Church, *the communion of Saints*, the forgiveness of sins, the resurrection of the body, and life everlasting. Amen.

As could be seen, the phrase "*Creator of heaven and earth*", had been inserted only in the seventh century, as well as the phrase "*He descended into hell*", the "*Catholic*" Church and the "*communion of Saints*".

The testimony (Creed) of the apostles is of great historical and dogmatic importance as it is the earliest witness on the beliefs of Jesus disciples and the early Christian Church.

5. F. The spread of Christianity until the declaration of Milan in AD 313

The Christian faith spread during the life of Jesus to parts of Palestine and after his resurrection to many parts of Syria and the Roman province of Arabia (present day Southern Jordan), and established a strong presence in Antioch in Northern Syria (which was one of three greatest cities of the Roman Empire), to which Peter, Paul and Barnabas and other disciples of Jesus had to flee after the persecutions endured in Jerusalem at the hands of the Jewish religious authorities, and the sack of Jerusalem by the Romans in AD 70. It was in this city that Apostle Peter established his first episcopate and all future missionary travels of the apostles to Cyprus, Asia Minor, Greece, Mesopotamia and Persia took off from this city. These travels contributed to the spread of the new faith into many regions of the Roman Empire, especially at the hands of Apostle Paul, who was a Roman citizen and had good Greek language oratorical skills. Also due to the efforts of Apostle Peter and the other apostles who spread the new faith to Mesopotamia, Arabia, and parts of the Persian Sassanid Empire.

At the beginning, the Christian faith spread in between the Jewish communities of the Roman cities, but also in Mesopotamia and Persia, especially after the destruction of the second temple by Titus in AD 70, and the Jewish Rebellion of Bar Kokhba in AD 132–136 with the dispersal of Jews from Judea and Samaria. Also it spread between the poor subject peoples and the slaves of the Roman Empire and some intellectuals, amongst whom is Justin, Martyr (died AD 165 in Rome), a Christian Palestinian Greek from Neapolis (present day Nablus) imbued with the spirit of Greek Philosophy. As a Platonist, he thought about God and drew attention to the Jewish Prophets. By his writings, he tried to rebut the charge that Christians were disloyal to the Roman Empire. Justin's rational Christianity provided a revelation of the Divine Reason in which Socrates, Plato, but also the Hebrew prophets had partaken, which was only complete in Christ.

Others followed a similar line notably Titus Flavius Clemens (AD 150–215), known as Clement of Alexandria. He was an educated man influenced by classical Greek Philosophy, and in particular by Plato, to a greater extent than any other Christian thinker of his time. He believed that by using reason, a person could find the absolute Good and the Truth that is God. In one of his works he argued that Greek philosophy had its origin among non-Greeks and of the possibility of Jewish influence on Plato. Among his pupils was Origen from Alexandria.

Origen (AD184/185–253/254) was a teacher in a school for priests in Alexandria. He was a prolific Greek language writer in multiple branches of theology, including textual criticism, biblical exegesis, philosophical theology, and spirituality. He helped define Christian doctrine and promote Christian faith in Greek style philosophical work. Unlike many church fathers, he was never canonized as a saint because some of his teachings directly criticized the work of certain gospel writers. Origen was posthumously condemned as a heretic by a council at Alexandria in the year AD 400. In AD 543, Emperor Justinian again condemned him as a heretic and ordered all his writings to be burned. Another pupil of Clement was Eusebius of Caesarea, the author of the *Ecclesiastical History*.

The missionary zeal of Apostle Paul met acceptance amongst the gentiles, especially after the ruling of the first synod in Jerusalem (AD 49) stating that non-adherence of gentiles to circumcision is not a prerequisite for salvation, but only their abstention from eating blood, consuming meat offered to idols, and meat of strangled and dead animals.

As Christians were worshiping a single God like the Jews, The Romans looked at them with suspicion as they expected Roman citizens to worship Roman deities and sacrifice to the emperors as gods, beliefs and acts the Christians refused to perform. Due to the spread of Christians amongst the various peoples of the empire, unlike the Jews who were exempt from this worship and had a special status, the Roman emperors were not inclined to allow this religion to spread amongst the other nations and looked at the Christian faith as a threat to the cultural unity of the empire. Especially when faced with the disparity between the Roman culture with its violent nature, slavery, discrimination between free Roman citizens and the remaining subject peoples and slave populations, and the teachings of the Christian Church, which called for the worship of a single Loving and Merciful God, taught love, tolerance, equality and good relations between all humans. The first persecutions were started by Emperor Nero in AD 64, who seeking a scapegoat for a great fire in Rome proclaimed that Christians were its initiators. St Peter and St Paul perished during this period according to popular Christian tradition. More took place under emperors Trajan, Marcus Aurelius, Septimus Severus, Aurelian, Maximin and Decius (who some say persecuted the Christians to counter his predecessor, Philip the Arab's sympathy towards the Christians), Valerian whose savagery exceeded that of his predecessor, and Diocletian. During the rule of the later, and during a period of ten years, more than ten thousand Christians were killed in Egypt alone.

After the spread of the new faith across the Roman Empire, fed by the martyrdom of thousands of Christians, and the rally of many influential and powerful Roman citizens to the new faith, came the Edict of Milan in AD 313, which granted freedom of belief to all Roman subjects, followed by Emperor Constantine's conversion to Christianity and its adoption as the Empire's new faith, to give the Christian churches the right of outright freedom to proselytize peoples across the territories of the Roman Empire.

5. G. The apocrypha evangels

During the four centuries after the birth of Christ, many manuscripts were composed to set down in writing the life and teaching of Jesus, and preserve it for posterity. As many of these writings didn't report these events in a logical and objective way and were not up to the required degree of confidence, the early Christian communities didn't trust all of them, but only some. Accordingly and starting from the second century AD, an oral tradition based on the close relationship of each author to the disciples of Jesus was built in order to prove the correctness of the book.

The approval of the canonical evangels took more than a century and the final agreement on the canonical writings was not completed until the fourth century AD.

Starting from the end of the second century AD, we come across different writings that tried to fill up the voids of certain canonical evangels, mostly related to the childhood of Mary and Jesus, and the missionary work of Jesus disciples.

The contents of some of these manuscripts are difficult to believe, so that even the least discerning reader could discover their falseness.

A classification of the apocrypha evangels was made in *The History of religious thought of the Church Fathers* written by: Bishop Kyrilos Salim Pesters, Father Hanna Al-Fakhouri, Father Joseph Al-Absi Al-Boulisi, published in Arabic by the Catholic Press, Lebanon in 2001 as follows:

A   The evangels that are based on the original: The "Evangel of Peter" and the "Evangel of Jacob the First".

B   The Nazarean Evangels: to which belongs the "Evangel according to the Hebrews" and the "Evangel of the Ebionites". These two evangels are close to the Evangel of Matthew, and preserve Jewish traditions.

C The false evangels of the Gnostics as that of Thomas and Bartholomew and others.

The Evangel of Jacob the First shed the light on the Virgin Mary's childhood until her pregnancy and how her parents had pledged her to God in Jerusalem's Temple until she was 12 years old, when Joseph, who was widowed with grown children, took her under his protection. Also how Angel Gabriel announced her pregnancy with Jesus while she was a virgin. The First Evangel of Jacob was highly regarded and in use by the East Christian Greek (more than thirty manuscripts), Syrian, Armenian and Arabic churches during a long period of time. Around year AD 500, the Latin Church declared the Evangel of Jacob the First apocryphal, basing its decision on the writer's ascription of half-brothers to Jesus, while the Latin Church's interpretation of Jesus brothers (in Matthew 12: 47 for example) is that Jesus had only cousins.

The Evangel according to the Hebrews written in Aramaic language but with Hebrew letters was used by the Nazarenes in Southern Syria and Arabia and many researchers think that it is the original Aramaic text of the Evangel of Matthew. It is similar to the Evangel of Matthew and was used by the Aramaic speakers in Palestine and Syria. The Nazarenes are Christians of Jewish origin that did not abandon certain commandments of Moses' Law.

The Evangel of Barnabas was written by a Christian Italian convert to Islam in the fourteen century. The original Evangel of Barnabas, mentioned in a Greek collection of manuscripts, is lost.

5. H. Christian sects during the first five centuries AD

As mentioned in 5. G, there were many manuscripts related to the life and teachings of Jesus during the first four centuries AD, some approved by the Christian Church as canonical and others considered apocrypha, besides the epistles and other writings by the Church Fathers, written mostly in Greek but also in Aramaic in Syria and Mesopotamia. The cities of Alexandria and Antioch had their distinctive and contrasting schools regarding the interpretation of the Old and New Testament.

With the passage of time and due to many reasons, including the cultural heritage, the political situation but also personal interests, many Christian sects made their appearance especially in Egypt, Syria, and Asia Minor.

The theological school of Antioch, from the start, taught that God is one and concentrated on the humanity of Jesus Christ. Jesus was born, developed and died as any human, as per (Luke 2: 52: "And Jesus advanced in wisdom and age and favour before God and man."), meaning that he developed in thought and wisdom like any human, unlike God. But *He had two **origins**: divine as he didn't have a human father but was conceived by the Holy Spirit, and human being born from the Virgin Mary.*

At most, in the Evangels of Matthew, Mark and Luke, we find them calling him: "The Christ Son of the Living God" (Matthew 16: 16), (Mark 8: 29) and we find Jesus always calling himself "Son of Man".

We can deepen our search about the nature of Christ, based on (Matthew 23: 8–11: "As for you, do not be called 'Rabbi'. You have but one teacher, and you are all brothers. Call no one on earth your father; you have but one Father in heaven. Do not be called 'Master'; you have but one master, the Messiah. The greatest among you must be your servant".).

Also, Matthew wrote about Jesus calling out to God close to the time of his death on the cross as in (Matthew 27: 46: "And about three o'clock Jesus cried out in a loud voice, "*Eli, Eli, lema sabachthani?*" which means, "My God, my God, why have you forsaken me?"). We understand from this call that God is also the God of Christ.

Also, we read from the epistle of Apostle Paul to the Church of Ephesus, (Chapter 1 17: *"that the God of our Lord Jesus Christ*, the Father of glory, may give you a spirit of wisdom and revelation resulting in knowledge of him."). As we know, Apostle Paul wrote his epistles before most of the canonical evangels, accordingly he is a more reliable source than John the Evangelist.

Also, as we mentioned in Chapter 5 B above, regarding Jesus' answer concerning prayer, Jesus told his disciples to address God, our Father in Heaven, and not himself in prayer. And when Jesus asked the Pharisees about their opinion as to who the Messiah is, as in (Matthew 22: 42–45: "What is your opinion about the Messiah? Whose son is he?" They replied, "David's." He said to them, "How, then, does David, inspired by the Spirit, call him 'lord,' saying: 'The Lord said to my lord', "Sit at my right hand until I place your enemies under your feet?" If David calls him 'lord', how can he be his son?"), He demonstrated to them that he is not the son of David, (descendent of David) and that God is the Lord of Jesus Christ.

And when his disciples asked him about his return and the end of the world, he answered as in (Matthew 24: 36: "But of that day and hour no one knows, neither the angels of heaven, nor the Son, but the Father alone").

From all the above reported, it is clear that Jesus Christ confirmed that he is the "Son of Man" from the Virgin Mary and the "Son of God" from the Holy Spirit, and God's Word to the Human race. He never declared that He is God or equal to God.

Contrary to the teaching of the theological school of Antioch, the theological school of Alexandria based its view on

Chapter 1 of John's evangel, to prove that the Holy spirit of God incarnated the body of Christ, so that Jesus Christ is a God equal to His Father in substance, and accordingly he is eternal as his Father, from where came the idea of the Holy Trinity that says that God the father, God the Son and the Holy spirit are three different persons (icons) in God.

*

One of the most important Christian sects that developed in the fourth century is Arianism. Arius (AD 250–336) was a Christian priest who lived and taught in Alexandria Egypt in the early fourth century. He was a disciple of Saint Lucian of Antioch (a canonized saint of the Roman Catholic Church). He opposed the teaching of the theological school of Alexandria regarding the relationship between God the Father and the person of Jesus, saying that Jesus was not of the same substance as God the Father and that there had been a time before his birth when he did not exist.

Arius taught that Jesus called himself "Son of Man" in all evangels (including that of John), that he was born and died as all men, that he didn't exist before his birth, and therefore is not eternal as God the Father. That as "Son of Man" he couldn't have existed before his birth from the Virgin Mary, and that his existence started only after his birth. He tried to correct the relationship between God the Father, the Son and the Holy Spirit by submitting the Son and the Holy Spirit to God the Father in order to preserve the idea of the One God – the single start point of all that exists. This single start point, Arius assigned it to God the Father. He is the only eternal and has no beginning and no end, and He is the only one who was not born nor created, and is the only one who didn't develop and evolve with time. On the contrary the Son was born and was created, developed physically and mentally with time and is not eternal.

Arius teaching spread between the Christians in Syria, Palestine, Mesopotamia and Asia Minor, including many bishops. We find this belief sculpted on the entry doors of Syrian Christian houses dating from the fourth century: "No god but the One God" as per the scripture carved on the stone doorway of a house in the dead city of Refade close to the monastery of St Simeon (the Historical Antiochian Encyclopaedia of Father Dimitri Athanasiou 1st Book page 131). Discussions heated up between the ones siding with Arius and the other faction supporting the divinity of Jesus to such a degree that obliged Emperor Constantine, who wanted a single Christian faith to unite the empire, and after intervening ineffectually, to convene a synod in the city of Nicaea (Iznik in present day Turkey).

The First Ecumenical Synod assembled in 325 AD with the participation of 318 bishops, mostly from the eastern areas of the empire, and headed by Emperor Constantine, not taking into account his lack of knowledge on the subject, himself being a new convert to the faith. Each of the two sides exposed its view: The bishop of Alexandria Alexandros, from the faction upholding the divinity of Jesus Christ, and the priest Arius and Bishop Usebius of Nicomedia from the faction believing that Jesus Christ is not equal in substance to God the Father, that Jesus was born, created and not eternal as God the Father.

Emperor Constantine sided with the view of Bishop Alexandros about the divinity of Christ and the Synod condemned and excommunicated Arius. The Emperor ordered his exile and the burning of all his writings. The following creed known as the "Nicene-Constantinopolitan Creed" was adopted at the Second Ecumenical Council held in Constantinople in AD 381, as a revised version of the original Nicene Creed of AD 325. It reads:

"We believe in one God, the Father Almighty, Maker of heaven and earth, and of all things visible and invisible.

And in one Lord Jesus Christ, the only-begotten Son of God, *begotten of the Father before all worlds.*

Light of Light, very God of very God, begotten, not made, being of one substance with the Father; by whom all things were made; who for us men, and for our salvation, came down from heaven, and was incarnate by the Holy Spirit of the Virgin Mary, and was made man.

He was crucified for us under Pontius Pilate, and suffered, and was buried, and the third day he rose again, according to the Scriptures, and ascended into heaven, and sits on the right hand of the Father; from thence he shall come again, with glory, to judge the quick and the dead whose kingdom shall have no end.

And in the Holy Spirit, the Lord and Giver of life, **who proceeds from the Father**, who with the Father and the Son together is worshiped and glorified, who spoke by the prophets. In one holy catholic and apostolic Church; we acknowledge one baptism for the remission of sins; we look for the resurrection of the dead, and the life of the world. Amen".

*

The Catholic Nicene-Constantinopolitan Creed reads as follows:

"I believe in one God, the Father almighty, maker of heaven and earth, of all things visible and invisible.

I believe in one Lord Jesus Christ, the Only Begotten Son of God, born of the Father before all ages.

God from God, Light from Light, true God from true God, begotten, not made, consubstantial with the Father; through him all things were made. For us men and for our salvation he came down from heaven, and by the Holy Spirit was incarnate of the Virgin Mary, and became man.

For our sake he was crucified under Pontius Pilate, he suffered death and was buried, and rose again on the third day in accordance with the Scriptures. He ascended into heaven and is seated at the right hand of the Father. He will come again in glory to judge the living and the dead and his kingdom will have no end.

I believe in the Holy Spirit, the Lord, the giver of life, *who proceeds from the Father and the Son*, who with the Father and the Son is adored and glorified, who has spoken through the prophets. I believe in one, holy, catholic and apostolic Church. I confess one baptism for the forgiveness of sins and I look forward to the resurrection of the dead and the life of the world to come. Amen".

The Catholic Nicene Constantinopolitan Creed differs from the Eastern Orthodox Creed by the addition *"who proceeds from the Father and the Son"*.

By comparing the Nicene Creed with the Creed of the Apostles, mentioned in Chapter 5 E above, we find that the additions were that: *the substance of Jesus Christ is consubstantial and same (ομοουσιος) as that of God the Father, that he is God as is God the Father, that he was born but not created and accordingly eternal as God the Father and that through Jesus Christ all things were created.*

After less than three years, Arius was recalled from his exile after he agreed to enter a modification (added a single letter: i) to the Nicaea Creed stating that the Son's substance resembles (ομιοουσιος) the substance of God the Father. At the deathbed of Emperor Constantine, it was the Arian Bishop of Nicomedia Usebius who baptized him.

Arianism was adopted by the descendants of Emperor Constantine, and it spread across the territories of the Roman Empire until Emperor Justinian during the period AD 533–554 took harsh steps to suppress it, and arrested most of its bishops. But Arianism already had spread by the efforts of Bishop Ulfilas to many Gothic, Lombard, Vandal and other Germanic tribes up to about the seventh century when the Roman Church in the west was able to suppress it.

The result of the First Ecumenical Synod of Nicaea was the appearance of the first schism in Christianity due to existing differences between the three synoptic evangels of Matthew, Mark and Luke, the Apostles Creed and the Epistles on one side and John's Evangel on the other, and the inability of the bishops present in the Synod to resolve the problem by relegating John's Evangel to the other apocrypha evangels, or at least deleting from it any assertions that Jesus Christ (The Word) is God.

Arianism didn't disappear and had many followers amongst Semitic peoples in Syria, Asia Minor, and especially amongst Christians of Jewish origin who never believed in the Hindu idea of incarnation that entered the Christian faith through the Gnostic mystic religions. The Early Christians were mostly Jews, as Jesus' disciples were. After the adoption of the Nicene Creed, with the Trinity statement, and the assertion that God the Father, God the Son and the Holy Spirit were Gods, the conversion of Jews to the Christian faith stopped. In Judaism, The Messiah (Christ) is not another God, as God is one. The disciples of Jesus would not have followed him if he told them that he is God. He in fact never told them that, as per the evangels of Mathew, Mark and Luke.

At most he answered affirmatively when asked by the Chief Priest if he is the Messiah Son of God (Matthew Chapter 26: 63–64). It would have being better for the bishops at the First Synod of Nicaea to agree saying that Jesus Christ had two *origins*: divine being conceived by the Holy Spirit of God and Human being born from the Virgin Mary, and not to deal with the question of his nature, that only God almighty knows, for his birth was a miracle that no human logic could explain.

The adoption of the Nicene Creed had as a result the consecutive appearance of many sects in Christianity. Nestorius – the Archbishop of Constantinople (Syrian from the town of Germanicea – Germa in Arab historian sources – presently Marash in Turkey) taught that calling the Virgin Mary Mother of God *"Theotokos"* is an enormous mistake, as she is a human being created by God and cannot be his Mother, and giving her such a name could be understood that she is the Mother of God the Father, which is totally unacceptable, and cannot be equally the Mother of the Son of God if he is as eternal as God the Father according to the Nicene Creed. That she should be only called Mother of Christ *"Christotokos"*). He emphasized the humanity of Jesus, Son of Man saying that Christ consisted of "two natures and two persons." The human nature and person were born of Mary. The divine nature and person: the Word (*Logos*) were of God.

The teaching of Patriarch Nestorius brought angry protests from the Alexandrian clergy in Egypt who called for a second church synod that took place in Ephesus in AD 431. The result of that church synod was the excommunication of Archbishop Nestorius, the prohibition of his teaching and his exile to a village in the Egyptian desert where he died. His teaching (Nestorianism) spread to Mesopotamia that was under the rule of the Sassanid Persian Empire, between the Eastern Syrian Christians (Assyrians), taking later the name of the Eastern Church.

*

Also, Eutyches, an archimandrite at Constantinople, emerged with diametrically opposite views to those of Nestorius. Eutyches asserted that the divine nature of Christ (the Word) overwhelmed his human nature and the two natures were fused into one new single divine person: that of Christ – the incarnate Word. Eutyches denied that Christ was consubstantial with men. His opinions brought him the accusation of heresy in AD 448, leading to his excommunication in AD 449. The teaching of Eutyches found large support between the subject peoples and the clerical authorities of the Roman Empire in Egypt, Syria and Armenia, as they saw in it another mean of preserving the unity of God after the rejection of Arianism: the One God has incarnated a human body – that of Jesus Christ. Also, it was a way to prove that the East Roman clergy in Syria and Egypt were best placed to interpret the scriptures old and new, being the inheritors of the Christian religion founder Jesus Christ, not to mention the personal frictions between the heads of these eastern churches and the church authorities in the capital. Eutychianism was again rejected at the Council of Chalcedon in AD 451. Those who did not approve the edict of the Chalcedon Council were later accused of being Monophysites (single nature followers) and these included the Coptic Church, the Armenian Church, part of the Syrian Church under the influence of Bishop Jacob Baraday (apart from the Maronite Church) and the Arab Ghassanid Church in the Roman Arab Province. These churches separated from the Roman Official Church and were subject to persecution until the Arab Islamic invasion of these countries.

To summarize: the inability of the Church Fathers during the second and third centuries AD, *and especially the bishops present in the first Church Synod of Nicaea, to solve the problem by relegating John's Evangel to the other apocrypha evangels, or at least deleting from it any assertions that contradicted the three synoptic evangels of Matthew, Mark and Luke, the epistles and the Apostles Creed led to all the disagreements, Christological disputes and schisms that occurred in the Church later. God only knows the nature of Jesus, as his birth was a miracle no human logic could explain. All we can say is that the Virgin Mary gave birth to Jesus Christ who was conceived by God's Holy Spirit (an inseparable part of God's entity), and that He does not have a human father, and that he is God's Word to the human race. That God spoke through him to men directly without the means of an angel or any other mediator, and that God gave him an authority He didn't give to any other human, as He arose the dead, healed the sick, the blind and paralyzed, calmed the* storm, walked on the waters of Lake Tiberias, fed thousands of people at a heavenly table (the evangels and the Koran), and as per the Koran (Surah 3: 49: "Lo! I fashion for you out of clay the likeness of a bird and I breathe into it and it is a bird, by Allah's leave, I heal him who was born blind, and the leper, and I raise the dead, by Allah's leave...").

Further, that He was persecuted, suffered and was crucified under Pilate the Pontius, died and God raised Him from the dead, that He is the first living human in God's Paradise and the New Adam.

As we accept the presence of God who created the world from void, and the first man Adam by breathing into a human form made of clay (or into an evolved Homo Sapien?), we should accept the same regarding the birth of Jesus, when the Virgin Mary chosen by God conceived through God's Holy Spirit and gave birth to Jesus Christ.

The only persons whose interceding with God could be accepted, should be Jesus Christ and the Virgin Mary (who was purified and selected by God) and the twelve Apostles who were chosen by Jesus Christ. The Virgin Mary is the Mother of Jesus Christ and not the Mother of God who created her, and our prayer and adoration should only be addressed to God the Father, as Jesus taught us, and the correct Christian testimony of faith should be the Apostles Creed.

The Christological disputes in the Christian East, that historians came to call "Byzantine Endless Arguments" because there was no way to resolve them, led to the destruction and ruin that befell Syria's populations and grandiose cities, as reported by Father Dimitri Athanasios (*The Historical Encyclopaedia of the Antiochian Patriarchate*, 1st Volume pages 154–155, 1997 edition) speaking on behalf of Syria's ruined cities and addressing in the name of the Syrian people those responsible for its destruction: "Oh kings, rulers, governors, civil and religious spiritual leaders, God gave you the rule of a holy nation and a good nurtured people and a beautiful rich country. How many times we felt the danger of your ethnic, religious and ideological disputes on the people, and the dangerous results of fundamentalism and extremism leading to fanaticism, internal divisions and strife. The foreigners used these ethnic and religious disputes to weaken the country and submit it to their rule, making you a toy in their hands and controlling our fate. We didn't find in you but lust for power and tyranny. How many times we asked you to seek life for us and existence for yourselves, and not to be audacious seeking death to your people and ruin and occupation to your country... and asked you not to exert yourselves in dogmatic interpretations of no interest to your people, nor take extreme and complicated positions in religious and Christological matters as these dogmatic subjects might lead to uncontrolled reactions from the simple minded people leading to violence, persecutions and mass killings".

5. I. Christian churches from the sixth until the end of twentieth century

a. **Eastern Christian Churches till the Arab Islamic Invasions**

As mentioned above and following the decisions of the Chalcedon's Church Synod of AD 451, the following "Monophysite" churches separated from the Roman Official Church: The Coptic Egyptian Church, The Jacobite Syrian Church, The Armenian Church and the Church of the Ghassanid Arabs. The Nestorian Church had already separated after the Synod of Ephesos in AD 431.

As Egypt, Syria and Armenia were under Byzantine rule during the fifth and sixth centuries, the followers of these Eastern Churches suffered persecution by a number of Byzantine Emperors, the fiercest during the reign of Emperor Justinian (ruled from AD 527 till AD 565). As part of the Syrian Jacobite Church and the Nestorian Church (the Church of the East) in Mesopotamia were under Persian Sassanid rule, the Syrian Jacobite Church in Mesopotamia had to cut its ties with the Syrian Jacobite Archbishop of Antioch, in order not to be suspected of being an agent of the Byzantine authorities. In spite of that, Xerxes 1st, the king of Persia, led a campaign of persecutions against the Christians during the first half of the sixth century that left thousands dead which ended in AD 545. The activities of the Eastern Church extended to India (St Thomas Church – Kerala State), the Eastern coast of the Arabian Peninsula (Bahrain, Qatar and Oman), some Tatar and Mongol tribes in Central Asia and to China during the rule of the Tang Dynasty (from AD 618 to AD 906).

As for the Syrian Maronite Church, whose followers inhabited the regions of Western Syria, the Orontes river Basin up to the Taurus Mountains in the North, it remained under the authority of the Roman Official Church, having accepted the Monothelic Christological belief (belief in two natures of Christ with a single divine will) imposed by Byzantine Emperor Heraclius. Its relation with the Syrian Jacobite Church was under tension until and after the occupation of Syria by the Muslim Arabs in 642 AD.

b. **The Official Roman Church**

The existence of two capitals in the Roman Empire: Constantinople in the eastern part and Rome in the western part with two Roman Emperors and two competing archbishops caused with the passage of time the division of the Roman Christian Church. The eastern part of the empire was an area where the Hellenistic culture was dominant, where existed many cities that had an important role in the early spread of Christianity as Jerusalem in Palestine, Antioch in Syria, and Alexandria in Egypt, and where the Greek language was widespread and used by educated people. In the western part of the Empire with its old capital Rome, the Latin language was widely in use in the Italian Peninsula, Gaul, the Iberian Peninsula and the Province of Africa. There was fierce competition between these two parts of the Empire due to differences in their cultures that also reflected on church religious matters and leadership. As political power in the Hellenistic East was not pyramidal in shape and not concentrated in single hands due to the many ethnicities present in the area, and following a trend in the long history of these peoples that combined their ethnic entities with their religious beliefs (example: the Jewish, Egyptian, Assyrian and Armenian peoples), similarly each of them had its ethnic church with at its head a Patriarch: one in

Jerusalem, one in Antioch and one in Alexandria, besides the Patriarch of Constantinople.

In the western part of the Empire, no political and cultural centres rivalling Rome evolved historically, and accordingly this fact reflected on a concentration of religious power in the hands of the Pope of Rome, the inheritor of the first bishop of Rome – Apostle Peter. This competition between Rome and Constantinople, with the passage of time and the problems facing the translation of the evangels, and other scriptures from Greek to Latin led to differences in the interpretation of certain passages of the Bible, especially those regarding the origin of the Holy Spirit: Did He proceed from God the Father as believed by the Roman Orthodox Churches of the East or did He proceed from God the Father and God the Son as affirmed the Roman Catholic Church of Rome? But the biggest controversy between the two sides was the right of leadership of the whole Christian Church, as the Pope of Rome firmly believed that being the inheritor of Apostle Peter's bishopric, he had the right to lead the Church in both East and West.

These differences and other political factors led to the first schism between Pope Nicholas 1st and Fotius, the Patriarch of Constantinople in AD 863. These differences increased with the passage of time, especially after the sack of Constantinople by the Fourth Crusade in AD 1204, and the establishment of a Latin kingdom with a Latin Patriarch, that lasted 57 years. Later the Byzantine Empire recovered Constantinople and the Orthodox Patriarch returned from exile to his previous seat. These events led to the division of the official Roman Church to an Oriental Roman (Byzantine) Church which continued to call itself Roman Orthodox (straight Road) with a patriarch at each of its historical seats: Constantinople (the Ecumenical Patriarch being its nominal head), Jerusalem, Antioch and Alexandria, and another in the West that called itself Roman Catholic (Ecumenical) with at its head the Pope of Rome.

During the tenth and eleventh centuries, two Byzantine monks: Cyril and Methodius carried out missionary work amongst the Slavs of the Balkan Peninsula (Bulgarians, Serbians) that extended later to the other Slav peoples to the North: Russians, Ukrainians, Slovakians but also Valakhians (present day Romanians). Due to his knowledge of old Slavic language, Cyril created the Cyrillic Alphabet and translated the Bible to the Slavic language, thus creating the required conditions for the spread of Christianity to North-Eastern Europe.

c. **Eastern Christian Churches under Arab Islamic occupation**

After the conquest of Syria, Egypt and Mesopotamia by the Muslim Arabs in AD 642, many of its Greek residents and also some of its influential and wealthy Syrians escaped to the areas under Byzantine control in Asia Minor and Constantinople. Amongst those who left to Asia Minor were also the Ghassanid Arab King Jabla Ibn Al-Ayham and a number of his subjects. The patriarchal seats of the Byzantine Orthodox Church in Jerusalem, Antioch and Alexandria remained for a while unoccupied, while the Coptic and Jacobite Syrian Church followers remained not much affected by the Islamic occupiers for a while under the Omayyad Caliphs, as long as they paid the tribute. The Muslim Arab invaders, who remained a distinct minority in the conquered territories, formed an aristocratic military cast headquartered mostly in the town suburbs. They required the help of the local populations in the domains of administration, agriculture, industry and constructions, as they were nomads without any knowledge and experience in these fields.

The Christians of Syria, Egypt and Mesopotamia, as well as the Jews and Zoroastrians were tolerated as "People of the Scripture" whose head tribute and taxes supported the empire. The situation of the Christian populations of Syria, Egypt and Mesopotamia worsened at the end of the Abbasid Caliphate when law and order broke down. At the end of the tenth century the Caliphate controlled only a small area around the capital Baghdad. Its weakness encouraged the Caliphate's Seljuk Turkish troops to manipulate the Caliph and establish a number of Turkish vassal states in Persia, Iraq, Syria and Asia Minor, and their rulers started persecuting the large Christian populations still living in these countries. Also, Egypt in the tenth century came under the rule of the Fatimid caliphs (an Ismaili Shiite Sect), who were in general (Apart from Caliph Al-Hakem) tolerant towards their Christian subjects. The Christians, under the rule of the Turkish Seljuk rulers and the Fatimid Caliph Al-Hakem were forbidden to attend prayers and maintain/repair their churches, were obliged to wear special clothes to differentiate them from Muslims and foreign Christians were forbidden pilgrimage to the Holy Land, events that precipitated the crusades of the Christian Latin West.

d. **The Pope of Rome and the crusades**

The role of the Pope of Rome changed from pure religious to religious and temporal when he became a head of state of certain territories in the Italian Peninsula, following the Grant of Pepin "La Donation de Pepin", that was later approved by the West Roman Emperor Charlemagne in AD 774. In the following centuries the Pope came to be called the Representative of Christ on Earth "Le vicaire du Christ sur terre", and was the one who granted authority to kings and heads of states in the Christian West. After the occupation of Jerusalem by the Seljuk Turks and their persecution of Christian pilgrims, he called the heads of states of the European Christian West to free the Holy Land in Palestine, and rescue the Christians of the East from the Seljuk Turks, who took over Jerusalem in AD 1078 from the Fatimids, who until then allowed the pilgrimage of Christians to the Holy Land unhindered. Another of his aims was to unite the Christian Byzantine east and Latin West under his authority.

The aim of the Christian kings and princes of the European West, besides their religious zeal to free the Holy Land, was their wish to conquer and rule the rich lands of the Levant and the Byzantine Empire.

The crusades failed to establish Latin states in the Holy Land (present day Syria, Lebanon and Palestine) and Asia Minor, as the Byzantines recovered Constantinople from the crusaders in AD 1261 and the Mamelukes, the Muslim rulers of Egypt, recovered the last Crusader town of Acre in Syria in AD 1291. The relationship between the Christians of the Levant and the Muslims incurred further damage due to the Crusades, as the Christians were accused of helping the crusaders against their Muslim countrymen in Syria and Palestine, resulting in more persecutions by the Mamelukes after the defeat of the crusaders. The bad relations between the Orthodox Eastern Churches and the Catholic Latin Church, which led to the sack of Constantinople in AD 1204, and the lukewarm treatment of the Levantine Christians by the Crusaders, that was not much better than that of the Seljuk Turks, did not plead in their favour and alleviate their treatment by the victorious Mamelukes.

The same situation facing the minority Christian populations of Iraq and Syria by the Muslims of these countries, repeated itself after the "Crusade" carried out by the United States under President Georges Bush Junior in 2003 against Iraq, as the Christians were suspected of helping the crusading Americans against their fellow countrymen, leading to the emergence of the Islamic State in Iraq and Syria (ISIS), to mass killings and the immigration of most of the remaining Christians of the Middle East.

After the conquest of Constantinople by the Ottoman Turks in AD 1453 and their occupation of Syria and Egypt in AD 1516, the isolation of the East Christian Orthodox Churches from the Catholic Church increased.

e. **The Catholic Church Reformation**

The reformation of the Catholic Church started as a result of the Renaissance Movement in the Sixteenth Century, the invention of printing and the spread of scientific thinking. It started in AD 1517 by an Augustinian monk and Catholic Church Doctor: Martin Luther, when he nailed "The Ninety-Five Thesis" to the door of the castle church in Wittenberg – Saxony, declaring his opposition to the temporal earthly powers of the Pope of Rome, objecting to the manner the Pope used to collect money by selling indulgences, and opposing the held idea regarding the Pope's immunity from error. Also, he declared his opposition to the practice of the Virgin Mary's worship and the Church Saints intercession with God, to the oath of celibacy of the Catholic Church clergy preventing them from marriage, his opposition to monastic life and his opposition to the intercession of the Catholic priest between God and man. He explained that Jesus Christ didn't ask his disciples to abstain from marriage and selected his married disciple Peter to be the Honorific Head of His Church, but requested his disciples to actively spread the Evangel (Good News) to humankind. An excerpt from Apostle Paul's first epistle to the Church of Corinth follows (paragraph 9: 5: "Do not we have the right to take along a Christian wife with us on our travels as the other apostles do, and the Lord brothers, and Cephas?"). Cephas is the Aramaic name of Apostle Peter, meaning rock.

Martin Luther translated the Bible from Latin to German language, as the Catholic Church until then was using Latin Bibles in all of Germany, a fact that didn't help many people to understand it. He published it using the Gutenberg printer. The Reformation Movement required each believer to read the Bible now available in German language, and to understand it using a personal effort, even if that personal understanding contradicts certain teachings of the Catholic Church and its clergy.

The result of the Reformation Movement (Protestantism) was the establishment of Lutheran Churches in most of Germany and many other North European countries. The translation of the Bible to English language (King James translation) took place in AD 1611 and the Bible was later translated to many Scandinavian languages. Monasteries in North Germany and many North European countries shut down and monks and nuns dispersed. Missionary organizations of many reformed protestant churches were established that competed with Catholic missionary organizations in the spread of Christian Faith in Africa, Asia and America in the following centuries and till the present day.

f. **The Monastic Movement in Christianity**

The monastic life started in Egypt about AD 300, when Antonius left to the loneliness of the desert in Egypt for worship, followed by Pachomius who established the first monastery in the desert. The goal of the movement was to achieve individual perfection through seclusion, meditation, prayers, distancing one-self from worldly attractions and striving to get closer to God. The monastic movement spread to Syria, especially Northern Syria. Here a number of ascetics were active converting the pagan populations, amongst them was a certain monk by the name of Maroun. He didn't establish a monastery and didn't stay under a roof during harsh winters and hot summers, but went on foot from village to village between Antioch and Aleppo calling for the worship of a single God, preaching the Evangel. In his name was later founded the Maronite Syrian Christian Church. Also came to us the story of the monk Simon the Stylite who ended his life living on a column.

The movement thereafter moved to Asia Minor where monks formed extended monasteries and the movement grew to such an extent that bishop Basil the Great had to intervene and impose strict regulations and rules on these monasteries. After the Synod of Chalcedon in AD 451, and due to unrest and agitation created by monks meddling in the Church Christological Dispute, each church bishop had to supervise the life of monasteries under his jurisdiction.

The monasteries in the East after the Islamic invasions and under the rule of the Omayyad Caliphs and the first Abbaside Caliphs enjoyed the protection of the Muslim rulers acting according to Surah 5: 82 of the Koran, that called for the treatment of Christian priests and monks with respect. The monasteries became centres for spiritual and cultural guidance of Christian subject peoples during periods of instability. Their contribution in saving and translating the manuscripts and works of famous classical Greek authors is well known.

To the monasteries of the Syrian Christians in North Syria and Mesopotamia befell the honour of translating the works of Greek Philosophers, Physicians, Geographers and Mathematicians from Greek to Aramean, and later from Aramean to Arabic and thus their preservation to future generations. Many Syrians were fluent in Greek language having been for one thousand years under the Greek-Macedonian, Roman and Byzantine rule. Later, these translated works were translated from Arabic to European languages via Al-Andalus (Spain) during the European Renaissance.

The monastic life spread later to Western Europe. Several monastic orders were established during the Middle Ages: The Franciscan Order that swore an oath of poverty, chastity and discipline, the Dominican Order formed by the Pope of Rome to combat heresies, and the Carmelite Order having as goal seclusion and prayer, and many others.

The monastic movement historically was opposed by many Christian monarchs and rulers and as we mentioned above, by the Reformation Movement. Many historians believe that the demise of the Byzantine Empire and the takeover of Asia Minor and Syria by the Seljuk and Ottoman Turks – nomads from Central Asia, was partly due to the considerable increase in the number of monasteries that were exempt from taxation, where many young men thought to escape from military service and therefore didn't marry and rear children, which lead in time to changes in the population composition of these countries, especially taking into account that Muslim Arabs and Turks can marry up to four women . Other historians blame certain monks for the many heresies and disputes that plagued the body of the Christian Church in the East in the first five centuries.

More recently, we are witnessing cases of sexual harassment and paedophilia by some Catholic clergy and monks, widely spread via audio-visual means, that embarrass the Church and lead some Christians to distance themselves from the Church and pushed others to request from the Catholic Church authorities to allow priests to marry, in order to satisfy their human sexual needs, as was the case of the Early Church of Rome, and as is the present situation in the Orthodox and Protestant Churches and some Eastern Catholic Churches.

g. **The diminishing influence of the Catholic and Orthodox churches on Christians life at the end of the twentieth century**

We are witnessing the diminishing influence of the Catholic and Orthodox churches on the minds of their followers at the end of the twentieth century, especially in Western Europe. This could be attributed to the following factors:

1. The traditional way of interpreting the Bible by these two churches, inflexible dogmatism that did not take into account the development of sciences and general level of knowledge and social progress after the European Renaissance.

2. The Industrial Revolution of the nineteenth century and the feeling it created that by science and logical thinking, man could improve his life without having to rely on a better hypothetical afterlife.

3. The wars of the twentieth century in Europe and the resulting destructions, the death of tens of millions of people, mostly young men and the barbarity and hard feelings it generated in the hearts of millions of people that uprooted the feelings of love and mercy, compelling women to work in order to sustain their children, resulting in the dissolution of the family.

4. The influence of materialistic values on the minds of peoples of economically developed countries and the resulting race after money and material values that do not leave much time for parents to devote to their children.

*

The second and third factors mentioned above are facts that already have occurred and their results are impossible to reverse. The forth factor produced a loss of balance in the societies of economically developed countries between family values, ethics, fair relations in society and technical/technological development. This unbalance has already caused problems that the developed societies of the West are experiencing. One of these is the weakening of family ties, as parents don't have much time to spare for their children's education, as both have to work to satisfy continuously increasing material needs. Many married couples are not having children and many young men and women are not marrying. The populations of Western Europe are aging and decreasing in number. Cases of depression, hopelessness, stress and suicide are on the rise and individualism is taking hold. People are spending much of their time on electronic means of communications without having much human-to-human contact. These societies are ready for a spiritual awakening.

Here comes the role of the Church and its mission, but what role should it play now to reach the minds and hearts of the twenty-first century men and women? The transition of the Catholic and Orthodox Churches to institutions with employees – the clerics, whose interest is to earn their living conducting routine work for their institutions, without, for some of them, much thought given to their role as leaders of good example to society, assisting and helping the needy and participating in solving the problems of everyday life, not to mention the luxury surroundings of some senior clerics (example: the Pope of Rome and his suite and some patriarchs and archbishops of the Orthodox Church), and the dogmatism of its teaching that does not take into consideration the development of sciences and the recent level of knowledge, and the use of old forms of liturgy in old dead languages in church services (Latin and Old Greek) that are not understood by the believers, led many people to distance themselves from the Church.

The Reform Movement tried to fill-up the void created by the inertia of the Catholic and Orthodox Churches and are competing with these churches to reach the minds and hearts of Christians and others, by returning to the fundamental teachings of the Christian Faith using a modern logical mind to interpret the Evangels and the Old Testament. As previously explained, many Reformed Churches and many Christians agreed that the texts of the Old and New Testaments should not be understood as being emanating word for word from God and that there were hand copying mistakes before the invention of printing and some translation mistakes occurring over the centuries. For example, the evangelist Matthew starts his evangel by listing the genealogy of Jesus attributing it to King David through Joseph the husband of Mary as in (Matthew 1: 1–16: "... David.... and Jacob of Joseph, the husband of Mary, of whom Jesus was born, who was surnamed Christ."). The Evangelist Matthew himself in other parts of his evangel confirms that Jesus has nothing to do with Joseph and King David, as he didn't have a human father and was born from the Holy Spirit of God and the Virgin Mary. The Evangelist Matthew possibly wanted to prove the genealogy of Mary the mother of Jesus and originally in his evangel he had probably written the name of Mary instead of Joseph, but later, a scribe or translator made the mistake of replacing Mary with Joseph the husband of Mary.

Also, we read in the Evangel of (Matthew 5: 3: "Blessed are the spiritually poor, for theirs is the kingdom of heaven."). The translation from Aramaic to Greek and from Greek to English is poor and the sentence should probably read: Blessed are these who seek (or are in need of) the Spirit.... The same bad translation caused the following sentence in (Matthew 27: 51–53: "... the earth shook; the rocks were split; the tombs were opened and many bodies of the buried saints were raised and after His resurrection they left their tombs, entered the holy city and appeared to many."). This sentence contradicts Matthew himself and the other Evangelists, as according to them, the resurrection of all humans will happen only at the End of Time. It seems that the translator from Aramaic and/or Greek wanted to impress the audiences by this exaggeration.

In my opinion, if the Catholic and Orthodox churches keep their old dogmatic interpretation of the Bible, the Reformed churches stand a better chance to influence the hearts and minds of modern men and women.

Chapter Six

Islam

6. A. The Arabian Peninsula and the Hejaz region before Islam

Anthropologists consider the central plateau of the Arabian Peninsula and the Syrian Desert as the country of origin of Semitic peoples from where they started their migrations after the late ice age (after the eighth millennia BC) due to the gradual desertification of the country. These migrations took the form of consecutive tribal moves to the countries to the North of the Arabian Peninsula i.e. to Mesopotamia and Syria but also to the South, i.e. to Yemen and Oman. The North Semitic tribes: Akkadian, Amorites, Aramaic, Assyrian and Canaanite tribes left the central high plateau of Arabia and the Syrian Desert migrating to Mesopotamia and Syria, slowly mixing up with the Caucasian mountain peoples living in the southern flanks of the Zagros and Taurus mountains. The Semitic Arab tribes that remained in the Arabian Peninsula consisted of the North Arabian tribes that included the Adnan tribe and the South Arabian tribes that included the Qahtan tribe. References to Arab tribes were mentioned in Assyrian records of King Shalmaneser III (859–824 BC) and in Babylonian records of king Nabonidus (556–539 BC). Part of the South Arabian tribe of Qahtan after the destruction of the Ma'reb Dam in the second century AD, also migrated to the

North. The Ghassan branch settled in Southern Syria mixing up with the Nabatean Arabs and making Bosra their capital, while the Tanukh branch of the Qahtan tribe including the Banu Lakhm (Al-Manazira) migrated to Southern Iraq and made Al-Hira their capital.

The Hejaz area is located in North Western Arabia and its society consisted of settled North Arabian tribes (Aad, Thamoud, Nabat, Tasm, Umaim, Thaqif, Jarham, Khuza'a, Adnan and others) around the water points and oasis as Yathrib (present day Medina), Mecca, Khaibar and others, and nomadic Arab tribes wandering and following rainfall and pastures for their flocks of camels, sheep and goats.

The trade relations between the Roman Province of Syria and Yemen – these two ancient countries with a history in civilization, passed through the important cities of Hejaz: Mecca and Yathrib. The summer and winter caravans each year transported spices, myrrh, and other goods from Yemen to Syria and other parts of the Roman Empire and on their way back from Syria to Yemen transported textiles, glassware, olive oil, wine and other manufactured goods to the cities of Hejaz and Yemen. Mecca was an important trading centre on this caravan trail.

Besides its important role in trade, Mecca was an important religious centre as it contained the black stone – Kaaba pagan temple with its collection of idols, and the nearby Oukaz marketplace, where the poets from all Arabia came to compete in the art of expressing their thoughts and feelings in a subtle language, with verses and sentences rich in meaning and rhyme. The Arabs as desert dwellers excelled in the art of the word, which was the only one they possessed as they didn't had knowledge in the sciences and sedentary arts of other nations.

Most of the tribes of the Arabian Peninsula were pagans, worshipping idols made of wood and stone. The four most renowned gods they worshipped were: Manat, who was the oldest goddess, worshipped by Arabs, depicted by a statue on the Red Sea between Mecca and Yathrib. All the Arabs offered her presents and it represented destiny. The second was Allat, the goddess of fecundity, depicted by a white square stone worshipped by the Thaqif tribe. It was a replica of the mother goddess Ashtoreth worshipped by the North Semitic tribes. The third was Al-Izza, the goddess of the morning star, worshipped at the location of three palm trees in Wadi Nakhleh. The forth was Hubel and it was the most important idol of the Quraysh tribe. It was made of red agate and had its right arm broken when found. Quraysh made it a golden hand.

Certain Muslim historians believe that Ishmael, the son of Abraham from his slave woman Hagar, took wives from the North Arabian tribe of Adnan settled in Northern Hejaz, although other historians dispute it. They also relate that the tribe of Quraysh of whom was born Prophet Muhammad was a branch of the Adnan tribe, making Prophet Muhammad a distant descendant of Ishmael, the son of Abraham.

The South Arabian tribes including the Qahtan tribe migrated to Yemen and Oman due to the gradual desertification of the climate in Central Arabia. The Qahtan tribe subdivided later to the tribes of Himyar and Qahlan, and from that later originated the tribes of Ghassan and Lakhm that migrated after the destruction of the Ma'reb Dam in the second century AD to South Syria and Mesopotamia. The tribe of Himyar with the passage of time intermarried with African Kushite tribes from the western shores of the Red Sea.

6. B. Foreign cultural and religious influences in Hejaz until the sixth century AD

The trade relations between the cities of Hejaz and Southern Syria had, as a result, facilitated the spread of the religious currents of thought of the Ancient Near East to Hejaz, and especially the Jewish religion, as many Jews migrated to the cities of Hejaz after the first destruction of the temple of Jerusalem by the Babylonian king Nebuchadnezzar II in 587 BC, but mostly after the destruction of the second temple by Titus in AD 70. They had, in the city of Yathrib, Khaibar, Taimaa and others an important presence. Also, Jewish settlers were present in many cities in Yemen. Certain settled Arab tribes had converted to Judaism after their contact with the Jewish migrants.

After the birth of Jesus, Christianity spread to Palestine and the Roman Province of Arabia in Southern Syria by the Evangelist Matthew who preached to the Nabatean Arabs, according to certain sources, and by other disciples, including Apostle Paul who spent three years with the disciples of Jesus moving between Damascus, Bosra and Petra (where it is said he learned the art of weaving tents).

After the conversion of Roman Emperor Constantine to Christianity in the fourth century and the proclamation of Christianity as state religion, and as mentioned in Chapter 5. H, differences in opinions broke out regarding the nature of Christ: Arius, a priest of Libyan origin who lived and taught in Alexandria, Egypt opposed the teaching of the theological school of Alexandria regarding the relationship between God the Father and the person of Jesus, saying that Jesus was not of the same substance as God the Father and that there had been a time before his birth when he did not exist, and therefore he was created by God. He was opposed by the bishop of Alexandria Alexandros upholding the full divinity of Jesus Christ and that he is God as is God the Father, that he was born but not created and accordingly eternal as God the Father.

The First Ecumenical Church Synod assembled in AD 325 in Nicaea sided with the opinion of Bishop Alexandros, and adopted the Nicaea Creed affirming that Jesus Christ was born of the Father before all ages, that he is very God of very God, begotten not created, being of one substance with the Father, by whom all things were made.

The opinion of Arius was declared heresy. He was excommunicated, exiled and all his writings destroyed but his opinion was supported by many bishops and his teaching spread to many parts of the empire including the Roman Arab Province.

The adoption of the Nicene Creed had as a result the appearance of other Christian sects. Nestorius – the Archbishop of Constantinople (Syrian, from the town of Germanicea – Germa in Arab historian sources) taught that the Virgin Mary Should be called only Mother of Christ and not Mother of God as she is a human being created by God and cannot be his Mother. The teaching of Patriarch Nestorius provoked a second church synod that took place in Ephesus in AD 431. The result of that church synod was the excommunication of Archbishop Nestorius, and his exile to a village in the Egyptian desert where he died. His teaching (Nestorianism) spread to Mesopotamia that was under the rule of the Sassanid Persian Empire, between the Eastern Syrian Christians taking later the name of the Eastern Church.

Eutyches, an archimandrite at Constantinople, emerged with diametrically opposite views to those of Nestorius. He taught that Christ had only a divine nature. This sect found large support amongst the Roman subject peoples and the clerical authorities in Egypt, Syria and Armenia, as they saw in it another mean of preserving the unity of God after the rejection of Arianism: the One God now has incarnated a human body – that of Jesus Christ. This opinion was again rejected at the Church Synod of Chalcedon in AD 451. Those who did not approve the Chalcedon Council decisions were later accused of being Monophysites (single nature followers) and these followers included the Coptic Egyptian Church, the Armenian Church, part of the Syrian Church and the Arab Ghassanid Church in Southern Syria. These churches separated from the Roman Official Church and were subjected to persecutions.

Starting from the second century AD, Christianity spread into the Eastern coast of the Arabian Peninsula at the hands of Christian missionaries from Mesopotamia, so that an Episcopal Seat was present in Qatar in AD 220 and another one also in Oman. The Monk, Abd Yashoo, spread the Christian faith in Bahrain at the end of the fourth century. After the Chalcedon Church Synod in AD 451 and due to the relations of these churches with the Church of the East, that was under Persian Sassanid rule, the Nestorian Christian Sect found acceptance by the populations of these areas.

Historical research established that: In Yemen, the first attempts to spread Christianity were at the hands of an Arian Christian mission sent by Byzantine Emperor Constantius II to the Hymiarite King in year AD 360 and therefore Arian Christianity was the first to appear in Yemen. During the fifth and sixth centuries, and after the conquest of Yemen by the Ethiopians, who were Monophysites, they encouraged the Monophysite Christian sect to spread, especially in the province of Najran. After the Persian conquest of Yemen from the Ethiopians, the Persians who were religiously tolerant didn't try to impose their own pagan religion, but allowed the Nestorian Christian sect that was widely spread amongst their Christian subjects in Mesopotamia and the Eastern coast of Arabia to take hold in certain areas of Yemen. Accordingly, due to succeeding historical events, all three Christian sects: Arian, Nestorian and Monophysite were present in Yemen, a fact that weakened them.

In the central part of the Arabian Peninsula (Najd and Yamama), recent archaeological discovery of stone carvings proved that Hind, the eldest daughter of Al-Harith – the king of Kinda established a Christian monastery in the sixth century.

To resume, by the fifth century AD, Christianity had spread between the Arabs living in Southern Syria (Nabateans and Ghassanids) and Mesopotamia (Manazirahs), evangelized by Jesus disciples, as was the case for Apostle Matthew, Paul, Thomas, Agapos, Sila and others. These apostles, and later clerics, monks and holy men were thought to be guided by the Holy Spirit.

The Old Testament and the Gospels that were written originally in Aramaic (Syriac), Hebrew and Greek languages were later translated into Arabic and written into an Arabised Syriac alphabet by the Arab tribes living in Mesopotamia and Southern Syria. Besides the Bible, these Arabic Christian texts included church prayers, essays about the delights in paradise for the good and the suffering in hell for the damned, like those written by Saint Ephrem the Syrian – Episcope of Nissibis, that resemble so strikingly the Koran surats describing the delights in paradise. These Christian texts also covered the life of Arab holy men as those of Hood, Saleh and Shueib.

It is noticeable here to mention that the numbering system used in the Syriac and later translated Arabic Bibles was an old Syriac numbering system. Syriac letters were used in numbering the Bible chapters (the first 10 letters of the Syriac alphabet were used for number 1 to 10, the 11th letter for number 20, etc...) which could give an explanation to the "mysterious" letters present at the start of certain surahs of the Koran (Surat Ya Sin, Surat Sad...etc...).

In the Hejaz area, the spread of Christianity although less evident than between the Arabs of the Fertile Crescent, was still noticeable. The uncle of Khadija Bint Khouelid – the first wife of Muhammad, Waraka Ibn Naoufal was an Arian Christian priest and that assumes that there was a Christian church in Mecca with believers. It was logical that he had a copy of the Arabic bible at his disposal, besides other liturgical texts, although certain Muslim historians (Al- Bukhari) believe that he himself read the Bible in Hebrew and translated it into Arabic.

There is a consensus nowadays that besides the priest Waraka Ibn Naoufal, people with known Christian faith included Oubeid Allah Ibn Jahsh (a Muslim who migrated to Ethiopia with his wife Oum Habiba, converted to Christianity in Ethiopia and died there during the life of Prophet Muhammad, as reported by Ibn Ishaq), and Othman Ben Al-Houaireth Ben Abdel Izza and others (Arab Christianity and its developments, Dr. Salwa Belhaj Saleh – Dar Al-Tali'a, Beyrouth 1997).

The Nasara (Nazarene) of the Koran were Arian Christians who followed Moses' Law, including circumcision and prohibition to consume certain foodstuffs.

6. C. Prophet Muhammad's life

Prophet Muhammad Bin Abdallah was born in this historical background in Mecca about year AD 571 in the tribe of Quraysh. He grew an orphan and was raised by Abdel-Muttaleb his grandfather and later after his death by his uncle Abi Taleb. With this later he travelled with the caravans owned by a rich widow: Khadija bint Khouailed to the Roman Province of Arabia (Southern Syria). Khadija finding him capable, wise and trustworthy married him, although she was about 15 years his elder. Early Islamic Arab sources acknowledge that her uncle the Christian priest (monk?) Waraqa Ibn Naoufal was also related to her husband Muhammad.

During Muhammad's multiple travels to Southern Syria, where the Arab tribe of Ghassan had settled few centuries ago in the Hauran area, to the east of River Jordan, he came into contact with its Christian inhabitants who were of different sects and ethnicities: Arians (followers of the sect of Arius who believed in the human nature of Christ), amongst whom was monk Bahira (his Aramaic name means: deep in knowledge), who met the young Muhammad and foresaw a brilliant future for him, the Monophysites who recognized a single divine nature in Christ, who had many followers amongst the Arab Ghassanid monks and clergy, and the Chalcedonian Greeks and Romans (the followers of the official Roman Church who believed in two natures in Christ: human and divine). All of them were in continuous quarrel.

Also, he met the Saba'ens – the followers of John the Baptist, and the Jews. His observations and the comparison of the life of the people in Roman Southern Syria with his own Arab people in Hejaz and the Arabian Peninsula, led him to conclude that his people were backward at different levels: spiritual, material, social, organizational and legal, as the Arabs were mostly nomadic tribes living on the margins of civilization in the steppes and deserts, worshipping a plethora of gods, building them wooden and stone idols, living in poverty without a steady income, depending on occasional rainfall to sustain their herds of camels, sheep, and goats, pushing the nomadic tribes in years of scarce rains to attack each other, and to plunder the populations of the oasis towns in order to survive.

He was deeply impressed by the civilized life of the Jews and Christians (People of the Scripture) based on the Old testament (Torah) and the Evangels, but later in his life (after his flight to Yathrib) especially by the Torah, that besides calling for the worship of a single omnipotent God, had the legal framework to organize the relations between people in society and covered the rules to follow in trade, taxes, inheritance, warfare, marriage, hygiene, food consumption, prayers and others. The Evangels of the Christians besides calling for the worship of a single God, opened the gates of salvation to all human kind and not only to the Israelites. It declared that the Messiah of the Old Testament had arrived, and that the Law of Moses in its minutiae is not any more required for one's soul saving.

From later events in his life and the "revelations" (especially from the Meccan Surahs), we deduct that young Muhammad was attracted to the Christian Arian sect taught by the priest/monk of Mecca: Waraqa Ibn Naoufal, the uncle of his wife Khadija and by monk Bahira, whom he met in the city of Bosra, who believed that the Messiah Jesus was created by God, and that he is the Spiritual Son of God being conceived by the Holy Spirit and His Word, as he didn't have a human father. Muhammad sided with its adherents who were persecuted by the official Byzantine authorities.

The sceptical and sensitive Muhammad, after reaching the age of forty, being faithful to his fifty-five years old wife Khadija, started feeling the need to seclude himself and retired often to a cavern close to Mecca (could it have been the shelter of his relative – Christian priest/monk Waraqa, where he might have studied with Waraqa the Bible and acquinted himself with certain Christian texts?), to meditate and compare the beliefs of his pagan and backward people with these of the Jews and Christians he met and contacted during his life. According to Muhammad, the Koran verses started being inspired and revealed to him by Angel Gabriel in that cavern (who requested him to read) in poetical rhyming style, and continued being revealed after a lull (could it be due to the death of priest Waraqa?) in a different style. The revelations continued being inspired after his flight to Yathrib but the style changed completely (the surahs are now lengthy and in prose), till his death (about AD 632) at the age of about sixty-two.

These "revelations" occurred during two major periods of his life: the first during his stay in Mecca until the death of his relative Christian priest Waraqa Ibn Naoufal, his wife Khadija and his uncle Abi Taleb during a period of about 12 years, and were called Meccan Verses. This period in his life was the most difficult for he was persecuted by his tribe Qureich who fought his belief in a single god as it contradicted the worship of the pagan gods whose centre of cult was in Mecca, with all what derived from the pilgrimage to Mecca in material and trade profits. His call during this period was peaceful, free from any legislative framework and from revelations calling to fight the unbelievers. It was limited to calls for the worship of a single omnipotent and merciful God.

The Meccan verses expose God's ways in rewarding the faithful and punishing the sinful and went into details in describing the Garden of Eden as earthly beautiful gardens full of all types of sensual pleasures, not too different, but more sensual, than a description of Paradise by the Syrian Christian bishop Saint Ephrem who lived two centuries earlier and wrote in *(Paradise Hymn XI: "Who has ever beheld such a banquet in the very bosom of a tree, with fruit of every savor ranged for the hand to pluck. Each type of fruit in due sequence approaches, each awaiting its turn: fruit to eat, and fruit to quench the thirst; to rinse the hands there is dew, and leaves to dry them with. There the springs of delights open up and flow with wine, milk, honey, and cream.*

No harmful frost, no scorching heat is to be found in that blessed place of delight; it is a harbour of joys, a haven of pleasures; light and rejoicing have their home there; gathered there are to be found harps and lyres. More numerous and glorious than the stars in the sky that we behold are the blossoms of that land, and the fragrance which exhales from it through Divine Grace. A river should flow forth and divide itself, except that the blessing of Paradise should be mingled by means of water as it issues forth to irrigate the world, making clean its fountains. Thus it is with another spring, full of perfumes, which issues from Eden and penetrates into the atmosphere as a beneficial breeze by which our souls are stirred; our inhalation is healed…" Paradise in the Qu'ran and Ephrem the Syrian by Theodore Janiszewski).

The Koran describe the Garden of Eden as consisting of a number of gardens as per *(Surah 55: 46 "But for him who fear the standing before his Lord there are two Gardens.")* and in *(verse 62: "And besides them are two other Gardens.")*.That makes the Garden of Eden consisting of four gardens. A description of the beauty of the gardens follows as per *(verse 66: "Wherein are two abundant springs.")*, and *(verse 68: "Wherein is fruit, the date palm and pomegranate.")*, and *(verse 70: "Wherein are found the good and beautiful.")*, and *(verse 72 "Fair ones, close guarded in pavilions.")*, and *(verse 74: "Whom neither man nor jinni have touched before the chosen ones.")*, and *(verse 76: "Reclining on green cushions and fair carpets.")*. And in *(Surah 39: 20: "But those who keep their duty to their Lord, for them are lofty rooms with other lofty rooms above, built for them beneath which rivers flow…")*. And in *(Surah 52: 22–23: "And We provide them with fruit and meat such as they desire. There they pass from hand to hand a cup wherein is no vanity, nor cause of sin.")*

And in *(Surah 56: 17–18: "There wait on them immortal youths. With bowls and ewers and a cup from a pure spring.")* and in *(verses 35–38: "Lo! We have created them a new creation. And made them virgins, lovers, friends, for those on the right hand.").* And in *(Surah 18: 31: "... theirs will be Gardens of Eden, wherein rivers flow beneath them; therein they will be given bracelets of gold and will wear green robes of finest silk and golden embroidery, reclining upon canopies. Blest is the reward, and fair the resting place."* and *in (Surah 47: 15: "A similitude of the Garden which those who keep their duty to Allah are promised: Therein are rivers of water unpolluted, and rivers of milk whose flavour does not change, **and rivers of wine delicious to the drinkers,** and rivers of clear run honey; therein for them is every kind of fruit...").*

On the other hand, the Meccan verses warn the sinners of the suffering in Hell and describe the punishment for the ones who disbelieve as in *(Surah 18: 29: "... Lo! We have prepared for the disbelievers Fire, which encloses them. If they ask for relief, they will be showered with water like molten lead which burns the faces...").* And in *(Surah 67: 6–8: "And for those who disbelieve in their Lord there is the doom of Hell, a hapless journey's end! When they are flung therein they hear the fire's roaring as it boils up, as it would burst with rage. Whenever fresh hosts are flung therein the wardens ask them: Did nobody warn you?")* and in *(Surah 44: 43–46: "Lo! The tree of Zaqqum, The food of the sinner! Like molten brass is boiling in their bellies...")* and in *(Surah 14: 49–50: "You will see the guilty on that day linked together in chains, their raiment of pitch... and the Fire covering their faces.")* and many other verses with very vivid descriptions, such as the following Medina verse in *(Surah 4: 56: "Lo! Those who disbelieve in Our revelations, We shall expose them to the Fire. As often as their skins are consumed, We shall replace them with fresh skins that they taste the torment. Lo! Allah is ever Mighty, Wise.").*

The Meccan verses were short, some of them with a rhyming poetical style that evolved in their build quality during the twelve years of Prophet Muhammad's stay in Mecca, and differ greatly in style with the later lengthy Medina verses. The gatherer of the Koran placed many Meccan Surahs and verses without chronological sequence in the middle and mostly at the end of the Koran. Many Meccan verses were mixed up with the later Medina verses in many of the Koran Surahs, when they were gathered later in a single volume during the Caliphate of Othman Ibn Affan around year AD 654, i.e. 22 years after Muhammad's death.

Due to the persecution of Muhammad by the Meccans, Muhammad and his followers had to flee from the hostile city of Mecca to the city of Yathrib in AD 622 (called later the city of the Prophet or Medina), after he concluded an alliance with two Arab tribes of this city: the Aous and Khazraj tribes, who in their turn had problems with neighbouring Jewish tribes who inhabited the city of Yathrib.

We discern a clear change in the mentality and behaviour of Prophet Muhammad after his migration to Yathrib, possibly due to his new contacts with the Jewish Rabbis of Yathrib, and the stronger influence of the Torah, as gone was the peaceful call to convert the pagans, in accordance with the Christian belief of priest Waraqa Ibn Naoufal, and his dedication to monogamy that he kept up to the death of his (Christian?) wife Khadija.

Therefore we find revelations requesting him to fight his enemies, and other revelations allowing polygamy, himself giving the example by marrying eleven women during his ten years residence in Medina, apart from the captive women – the spoils of wars fighting the unbelievers, whom his right hand now possessed.

The revelations to Prophet Muhammad in Medina (called thereafter Medina verses) changed content, as a new phase of Muslim Arab State building has commenced (not unlike the

Israelite state built by king David and Solomon). We find in addition to the revelations calling for the belief in a single God, many others commanding the believers to fight their and God's enemies as in *(Surah 2: 216: "Warfare is ordained for you...")* and *(verse 244: "Fight in the way of Allah and know that Allah is Hearer, Knower"),* and many other surahs (see clause 6. D4). We find also other verses regulating the life of the new Muslim society, the new Muslim state relations with its neighbours and the way its wars had to be conducted. Prophet Muhammad was the head statesman, army general, founder and legislator of this new terrestrial state.

During his stay in Medina, conducting war against the tribe of Quraysh and forming temporary political alliances with other Arab and Jewish tribes, it was logical for the revelations to Prophet Muhammad to have sided with the decisions he was taking, although some of them contradicted previous ones, because as we know, in politics there is not a straight principled line to follow at different times and in variable circumstances: So we find many revelations at the early stages of his stay in Medina, when he was still quite weak militarily, treating his new Jewish neighbours in Medina friendly, turning for prayer (Qibla) towards Jerusalem, requesting his followers to treat Jews and Christians as allies and friends having similar beliefs. During the final stages in his victorious war against Quraysh, when he felt close to victory, and in order to make it acceptable for the Meccans to surrender, the revelation allowed him to change the Qibla from Jerusalem to the Al-Kaaba shrine in Mecca as in *(Surah 2: 144: "We have seen the turning of your face to haven for guidance. And now verily We shall make you turn in prayer towards a qiblah which is dear to you. So turn your face toward the Ka'bah...").* Later, after his victory over Quraysh and the consolidation of his hold on other Arab tribes of the Arabian Peninsula, we find the revelation requesting him to fight the Jews and the Christians if they don't convert to Islam.

The Koran verses were assembled in (114) Surahs containing a collection of Meccan and Medina verses in a chaotic non-chronological manner. The easiest way to discuss their subjects is to classify them as follows:

- Verses calling for the belief in a single God: Allah, his angels and messengers.
- Verses narrating the life of God's prophets, their teaching and derived lessons.
- Verses criticizing the "People of the Scripture" for distorting (altering) the Bible, calling them to convert to Islam.
- Verses calling to fight the disbelievers, polytheists and those Jews and Christians who don't accept the true religion of Islam.
- The Sharia Law covering:
    - Social matters: marriage, divorce, food consumption, clothing, hygiene rules, prayers.
    - Economical matters: Zakat, inheritance, tribunals, etc.
    - Methods to use with subjugated peoples, dealing with enemies, payment of tribute, plunder of women, Kharaj (land taxes), Khoums, etc.

6. D. The main subjects of Prophet Muhammad's message

6. D1 – Verses calling for the belief in Allah, his angels and messengers, similarities between the Koran and the Old Testament:

The Koran resembles the Bible – The New Testament in that its message is directed to all humanity, and differs from it by being also a state constitution – the Sharia Law. In this later aspect it resembles Moses' Law of the Old Testament. According to the Koran, certain Hebrew prophets were also kings, as King David and King Solomon were, and their constitution was a terrestrial one based on Moses' Law. Each of them ruled a state, married many women and fathered many children. The terrestrial state established by Prophet Muhammad and the Sharia Law of the Koran resembles in many aspects these Hebrew/Jewish states ruled by these prophets/kings, and is in sharp contrast with the Heavenly Kingdom preached by Jesus Christ described in Chapter 5.

The Koran's Sharia Law encompasses all aspects of religious, social, economic, juridical, and war and peace matters. For example, retaliation is demanded from Muslims as per *(Surah 2: 179: "And there is life for you in retaliation, O men of understanding, that you may ward off evil")*. The payment of tribute to be exacted from Christians and Jews is requested from Muslims as per *(Surah 9, 29: "Fight against such of those who have been given the Scripture as believe not in Allah nor the Last Day, and forbid not that which Allah has forbidden by His Messenger, and follow not the Religion of Truth, until they are obliged to pay the tribute, being brought low")* and in *(Surah 8: 69: "Now enjoy the booty you have taken as lawful and keep your duty to Allah. Lo! Allah is forgiving, Merciful.")* and *(Surah 48: 20: "Allah promised you much booty that you will capture, and has given you this in advance, and has withheld men's hands from you, that it may be a token for the believers, and that He may guide you on a right path.").* The above much resembles the clauses of Moses' Law in the Old Testament, made two thousand years before Muhammad, requesting retaliation as in (Leviticus 24: 17–21: "Whoever takes a human life shall surely be put to death… If anyone injures his neighbour, as he has done it shall be done to him, fracture for fracture, eye for eye, tooth for tooth; whatever injury he has given a person shall be given to him. Whomever kills an animal shall make it good and whoever kills a person shall be put to death."). Regarding payment of tribute and spoils of war as *in* (Deuteronomy 20: 10-14: "When you draw near to a city to fight against it, offer terms of peace to it. And if it responds to you peaceably and it opens to you, then all the people who are found in it shall do forced labour for you and shall serve you. But if it makes no peace with you, but makes war against you, then you shall besiege it. And when the Lord your God gives it into your hand, you shall put all its males to the sword, but the women and the little ones, the livestock, and everything else in the city, all its spoil, you shall take as plunder for yourselves. And you shall enjoy the spoil of your enemies, which the Lord your God has given you.").

The combination of "Sharia" state constitution laws in the Koran with the religious call for the worship of a single God gave the nomadic tribes of the Arabian Peninsula the necessary basis to build their first Arab State in history. Prophet Muhammad was the founder and legislator of this state, the initiator of its twenty-seven war campaigns lead personally by him during the last 10 years of his life. His efforts at unifying the Arab tribes and the prohibition at infighting between them, becoming members of a united Muslim Umma, had as a natural result the direction of their warlike efforts to conquer the territories of the settled and prosperous peoples of the Fertile Crescent to the North at first, and later finding out that the forces of the Persian and Byzantine empires were weakened by the long wars they fought against each other, they undertook the conquest of the Persian Sassanid empire and large parts of the territories of the Byzantine empire, during a period not exceeding 100 years.

The fourteenth century renowned Muslim historian Ibn Khaldoun in his *Introduction Book*, Chapter 21 described the Arab conquerors as follows: "They treat the conquered peoples as do carnivorous animals, and these invaders as are the Arab, Zinata tribes and others... are savages that do not have a homeland..."). He adds: "... a story told about Omar Al-Khattab, may God bless him, when he was elected Caliph reports him inciting nomad Arab tribes to invade Iraq saying: Hejaz cannot be for you but a base, and its people cannot offer you more. Go conquer the land God promised you in His book as inheritance...". The Koran's new "constitution – the Sharia Law" perfectly fitted the mentality of the nomadic Arab tribes, as war and plunder for them was a way of life. We can provide here two out of many verses of the Koran describing the nomad Arabs, as in *(Surah 9: 97: "The wandering Arabs are more hard in disbelief and hypocrisy, and more likely to be ignorant of the limits which Allah has revealed unto His messenger. And Allah is Knower, Wise.")*. And *(Surah 48: 16: Say to those of the wandering Arabs who were left behind: You will be called against a people of mighty prowess, to fight them until they surrender, and if you obey, Allah will give you a fair reward...")*. These wars of conquest in the seventh century AD by the Muslim Arabs constituted the last migration wave of the Semite tribes outside the Arabian Peninsula *until today*.

The Koran calls for the worship of a single God, creator of the universe and life, similar to the Bible's Old Testament, but the story of the creation of the first man and the life and conduct of the Israelite prophets are listed chaotically in different surahs of the Koran without any chronological order, in stark contrast to the Bible, where we find the story of the creation of Adam and Eve, of Noah and the flood, the life of the prophets Abraham, Isaac, Jacob as well as the story of Joseph and his brothers, Moses and the exodus from Egypt, reported in a systematic chronological way in the Genesis and exodus books of the Bible.

There are also many differences between the Old Testament and the Koran: In the Koran we find Prophet Abraham offering his son Ishmael from the slave woman Hagar as sacrifice *(Surah 37: 101–113),* while in the Bible, it is his son Isaac from his wife Sarah (Genesis 22: 1–12). No mention in the Koran of the sin committed by Lot, the nephew of Prophet Abraham, when drunk he committed incest with his two daughters according to the Bible (Genesis 19: 30–38), and no mention of the sin committed by Prophet Abraham on his way to Egypt, when he asked his wife Sarah to tell the Egyptians that she is his sister, out of fear for his life thereby Pharaoh seeing her beauty married her, and returned her to Abraham when he found that she was Abraham's wife (Genesis 12: 11–19).

We rarely find mentions about the Israelite Prophets sins in the Koran, apart from the sin committed by Moses *in (Surah 28: 16: "He said: My Lord! Lo I have wronged my soul, forgive me. Then He forgave him. Lo! He is the Forgiving, the Merciful."),* and the sin committed by Prophet/ King David in *(Surah 38: 24-25: "… And David guessed that We had tried him, and he sought forgiveness of his Lord, and he bowed himself and fell down prostate and repented. So, We forgave him that…").* In general, the Bible depicts the prophets as humans who commit sin and repent. In what concerns Prophet Muhammad, we find mentions of his sins in the Koran as in *(Surah 48: 1–2: "Lo! We have given you O Muhammad a signal victory. That Allah may forgive you your sin, that which is past and that which is to come…")* and in *(Surah 40: 55: "… Lo! The promise of Allah is true. And ask forgiveness of your sin…")* and *in (Surah 9 117: "Allah has forgiven the Prophet, the Muhajireen and the Ansar who followed him in the hour of hardship, after the hearts of a part of them had almost swerved aside, He turned unto them in mercy…").*

It is worth mentioning that in the Koran, in addition to the stories about the Israelite prophets, we find stories covering the Ishmaelite Prophets, not mentioned in the Bible as Prophet Saleh, Hood, Chou'eyb and Zou Al-kifl.

One major difference between the Old Testament and the Koran is that the enemy in the Old Testament that God commanded the Israelites to fight was an ethnic enemy, (Deuteronomy 20: 16–17: "But in the cities of these peoples that the LORD your God is giving you for an inheritance, you shall save alive nothing that breathes, but you shall devote them to complete destruction, the Hittites and the Amorites, the Canaanites and the Perizzites, the Hivites and the Jebusites, as the LORD your God has commanded…"), while in the Koran, the enemy that Allah commanded the Muslims to fight is a religious enemy who do not believe in Allah and his messenger Muhammad as in *(Surah 9: 5: "Then, when the sacred months have passed, kill the idolaters wherever you find them, and take them captive and besiege them and prepare for them each ambush….")*, and in *(Surah 9: 29: "Fight against such of those who have been given the Scripture as believe not in Allah nor the Last Day, and forbid not that which Allah has forbidden by His Messenger, and follow not the Religion of Truth, until they are obliged to pay the tribute, being brought low")*, and in *(Surah 9: 123: "O you who believe! Fight those of the disbelievers who are near to you, and let them find harshness in you, and know that Allah is with those who keep their duty unto Him.")* and many others listed below in clause 6. D4.

Muhammad called his followers to believe in one God: Allah, His angels and the Last Day, the messengers of Allah (Jewish and Ishmaelite prophets) and in Jesus Christ son of the Virgin Mary as in *(Surah 2: Verse 62, 87, 253)*, *(Surah 3: Verse 45, 49, 55, 84)*, and others. The effect that the message of Jesus left in the mind-set of Muhammad early in his mission in Mecca is clear in *(Surah 30: 2–5: "The Romans have been defeated in the nearer land, and they after their defeat will be victorious. Within ten years – Allah is the command in the former case and in the latter – in that day believers will rejoice in Allah's help to victory…."*). This Surah was revealed after the Sassanid Pagan Persians invaded Roman Syria whose inhabitants were Christians, entered the city of Jerusalem in AD 614 and destroyed most of the city including the Resurrection Church.

6. D. 2. The Koran and the New Testament – similarities and discrepancies

As we mentioned in clause 6. D. 1, there are similarities between the Old Testament of the Bible and the Koran and some discrepancies. We will concentrate in this Chapter on the similarities and discrepancies between the New Testament and the Koran related to the person of Jesus Christ, including his miraculous birth, The Holy Spirit, the nature of Jesus Christ and his resurrection.

The Birth of Jesus:
The miraculous birth of Jesus son of Mary as provided in the Evangels and the Koran is very similar.

We read in the Evangel of (Matthew 1: 20-21: "But as he considered these things, behold, an angel of the Lord appeared to him in a dream, saying: Joseph, son of David, do not fear to take Mary as your wife, for that which is conceived in her is from the Holy Spirit. She will bear a son, and you shall call his name Jesus, for he will save his people from their sins.") and in the Evangel of (Luke 1: 28-31: "And he came to her and said: Greetings, O favoured one, the Lord is with you!). But she was greatly troubled at the saying, and tried to discern what sort of greeting this might be. And the angel said to her: ("Do not be afraid, Mary, for you have found favour with God. And behold, you will conceive in your womb and bear a son, and you shall call his name Jesus. He will be great and will be called the Son of the Most High.").

In the Koran, we read in *(Surah 3: 36: "... She said My Lord Lo! I am delivered of a female – Allah knew best of what she was delivered – **the male is not as the female**; and Lo! I have named her Mary, and Lo! I crave Your protection for her and for her offspring from Satan the outcast. And her Lord accepted her well and vouchsafed to her a goodly growth...")* and in *(verse 42: "And when the angels said: O*

Mary! Lo! Allah has chosen you and made you pure, and has preferred you above all the women of creation") and in *(verse 45: "When the angels said: O Mary! Lo!* **Allah Has given you glad tidings of a Word from Him,** *whose name is the Messiah, Jesus son of Mary, illustrious in the world and the Hereafter and one of those brought near Allah"),* and in *(verse 47: "She said: My Lord! How can I have a child when no mortal has touched me? He said: So* **Allah creates what He will. If He decreeth a thing, He says unto it only: Be and it is.").**

Until here, the birth of Jesus in the Evangels and the Koran looks similar: The Virgin Mary conceived her son Jesus from the Holy Spirit of God. But then, we read in *(Surah 19: 17–19: "And had chosen seclusion from them. Then We sent unto her Our Spirit and* **it assumed for her the likeness of a perfect man.** *She said: Lo! I seek refuge in the Beneficent One from you, if you are God-fearing.* **He said: I am only a messenger of your Lord, that I may bestow on you a faultless son.").** Here we distinguish a disparity between what the angel said in Surah 3: verse 47 and Surah 19: verses 17–19, as the Virgin Mary in this later verse thought that she is having intercourse with a perfect man, which contradicts the text in verse 47 or the Evangels, especially if we consider that the angels according to both the Bible and the Koran are spirits and not human beings that can marry and conceive children, and God does not need them to accomplish his creation.

The Holy Spirit:
As mentioned above in the Evangel of Matthew 1: 20-21, Angel Gabriel announced to Virgin Mary the birth of Jesus from the Holy Spirit of God. Also, we read in the Evangel of (Matthew 3: 16–17: "And when Jesus was baptized, immediately he went up from the water, and behold, the heavens were opened to him, **and he saw the Spirit of God descending like a dove and coming to rest on him;** and behold,

a voice from heaven said: This is my beloved Son, with whom I am well pleased.").

In the Koran, we read *in (Surah:2 87: "And verily we gave unto Moses the Scripture and We caused a train of messengers to follow after him, and **We let Jesus, son of Mary, to perform miracles and We supported him with the Holy Spirit**. Is it ever so, that when comes unto you a messenger with that which you yourselves desire not, you grow arrogant, and some you disbelieve and some you kill?").*

Also, in *(Surah 4: 171: "...**The Messiah, Jesus son of Mary, was only a messenger of Allah, and His Word which He conveyed unto Mary, and a Spirit from Him**....").*

Also *in (Surah 16: 2: "He sends the angels through the Spirit at His command unto whom He will of His bondmen...").*

Also in *(Surah 17: 85: "They are asking you concerning the Spirit. Say: The Spirit is by command of my Lord and of knowledge you have been vouchsafed but little.").*

All the above listed excerpts from the Evangels and the Koran confirms that Jesus Christ was conceived by the Holy Spirit of God and born from the Virgin Mary, and that Jesus didn't have a human father. That has been confirmed in the Koran as we find all references covering Jesus in the Koran calling him Jesus son of Mary, his mother only.

The author of this book and its translation into English being a person whose mother tongue is Arabic was surprised while reading the English translation of the *Meaning of the Koran* by Muhammad Marmaduke Picktahll, published by Dar Al-Kitab Al-Masri – Cairo 1970, to find that Mr. Picktahll has confounded the Holy Spirit with angel Gabriel having discarded *(Surah 16: 2 that says: "He sends the angels through the Spirit at His command...")*, which means that the angels are not the Spirit (Holy Spirit of God). Also *(Surah 97, 4: "The angels and the Spirit descend therein, by the permission of their Lord, with all decrees.")*, which again means that the Holy

Spirit is not an angel. I hope Muslims reading his English translation wouldn't make the same mistake.

Jesus Christ the Son of God:
At most, Jesus accepted the answer of his disciples when he asked them about their opinion of who he is, as per the response of Peter (Matthew 16: 16: "Simon Peter replied: You are the Christ, the Son of the living God."). We find the same answer in (Mark 14: 61–62). At another place and time, after his arrest, and questioning by the Jewish Grand Rabi, he answered as per (Matthew 26: 63–64: "And the high priest said to him: I adjure you by the living God, tell us if you are the Christ, the Son of God. Jesus said to him: You have said so. But I tell you, from now on **you will see the Son of Man** seated at the right hand of Power and coming on the clouds of heaven.").

In the Koran, there are many verses covering this subject. So *in (Surah 2: 116: "And they say: Allah has taken unto himself a son. Be He glorified! Nay, but whatsoever is in the heavens and earth is His. All are subservient to Him.").* Also, *in (Surah 18: 4: "And to warn those who say: Allah has chosen a son."),* also *in (Surah 19: 35: "It befits not the Majesty of Allah that He should take unto Himself a son. Glory be to Him! When He decrees a thing, He says unto it only: Be! And it is.").*

But the above verses contradict *(**Surah 39: 4: "If Allah wanted to have a son, He could have chosen one from amongst the people He has created.** Be He Glorified! He is Allah, The One, The Absolute).*

This last verse (Surah 39: 4) agrees with the belief of the Arian Christians (priest Waraqa Ibn Naoufal and monk Bahira who were Prophet Muhammad's mentors), as they believe that Jesus is the Son of God conceived by the Holy Spirit of God, born from the Virgin Mary but created by God, in contradiction with many other Trinitarian Christian sects who believe that

Christ is the non-created Son of God and therefore he is God besides God the Father and the Holy Spirit.

The Death of Jesus and his resurrection:
The belief of many Muslims is that Jesus Christ was not killed and didn't die, basing their belief on *(Surah 4: 157–159: "And because of their saying: We slew the Messiah, Jesus son of Mary, Allah's messenger – **they slew him not nor crucified him**, but it appeared so unto them… they slew him not for certain, **But Allah took him up unto himself…** There is not one of the People of the Scripture but will believe in him before his death…").*

This Surah contradicts *(Surah 3: 55: "**When Allah said: O Jesus! Lo! I am allowing your death and taking you up to me** and cleansing you of those who disbelieve and I am setting those who follow you above those who disbelieve until the day of Resurrection…").* And it contradicts *(Surah 19: 33: "**Peace on me the day I was born, and the day I die, and the day I shall be raised alive!**"),* but also *(Surah 2: 87: "… **We gave unto Moses the Scripture… and We gave unto Jesus, son of Mary clear proofs and We supported him with the Holy Spirit.** Is it ever so that when there comes unto you a messenger with that which you desire not, you grow arrogant, **and some you disbelieve and some you kill?**").*

The Last Surahs confirm that Jesus died and was resurrected by God, as per the four canonical Evangels and the belief of the Christians. The difference between Muslims and Christians is how Jesus came to die, as the Christians believe that Jesus died on the cross.

Is Jesus Christ God?
As we mentioned in Chapter 5 Clause H above, After the Church Synod of Nicaea in AD 325, and especially after the Church Synod of Chalcedon in AD 451, many sects appeared in the Christian Church: Arianism that believed in the human

nature of Christ, the Single Nature Sect (Monophysite Sect) that believed in a sole divine nature in Christ, besides the Official Roman Church belief in a dual divine and human nature in Christ: a divine nature being conceived by the Holy Spirit of God, and a human nature, being born from the Virgin Mary.

Due to many political, cultural and personal factors, the Coptic Church in Egypt, The Syrian Jacobite Church in Syria, the Armenian Church and the Church of the Ghassanid Arabs in Southern Syria adopted the belief in a single divine nature in Christ (the Monophysite Sect), basing their belief on John's Evangel. The Byzantine emperors persecuted the followers of this sect, as they did previously against the followers of Arius, the persecutions continuing until the advent of the Arab Islamic invasions of Syria, Iraq and Egypt.

Arians as we explained previously believed that Jesus Christ was created by God, although He had two *origins (not natures)*: humane and divine, and that God has chosen him as his son.

The Koran fought Monophysitism and the followers of that sect as per *(Surah 5: 17: "They indeed have disbelieved who say: Lo! Allah is the Messiah, son of Mary…")*, we find the same verse in (Surah 5: 72). We find the essence of what was said about the nature of Christ in the Koran *in (Surah :, 171: "O people of the scripture! Do not exaggerate in your religion nor utter aught concerning Allah save the Truth. **The Messiah, Jesus son of Mary was only a messenger of Allah, and His Word, which He conveyed unto Mary, and a Spirit from Him. So believe in Allah and his messengers and say not three – Cease! It is better for you – Allah is only One God.** Far is it removed from His Transcendent Majesty that He should have a son.")*. It sides with Arianism as per *(Surah 39: 4: **"If Allah wanted to have a son, He could have chosen one from amongst the people He has created"**. Be He Glorified! He is Allah, the One, the Absolute)*.

Certain historians believe that the decision of the Church Synod of Nicea in AD 325 was the main cause that lead to the appearance of Islam. At the start of Islam's appearance, many Byzantine clergymen tended to believe that the call of Prophet Muhammad was but a Christian heresy of the Arab Arian Church.

6. D 3. Prophet Muhammad's call to the People of the Scripture:

Prophet Muhammad tried to persuade the People of the Scripture that he is a messenger of God, as were the previous prophets of Israel, as *per (Surah 3: 84: "Say: We believe in Allah and that which is revealed unto us and that which was revealed unto Abraham, and Ishmael and Isaac and Jacob and the tribes, and that which was vouchsafed unto Moses and Jesus and the prophets from their Lord. We make no distinction between any of them, and into Him we have surrendered.")* and (Surah 2: 253: *"Of those messengers, some of whom We have caused to exceed others, and of whom there are some unto whom Allah spoke, while some of them He exalted above others, and We allowed to Jesus , son of Mary, to perform miracles and We supported him with the Holy Spirit..."*).

Also, at the beginning of his call (in Mecca), in order to show to his doubting pagan compatriots that his call was from God (Allah in Arabic) Prophet Muhammad used as witnesses the Israelites to prove that his call is from the true God as per *(Surah 46: 10: "Say: Consider if it is (the Koran) from Allah and you disbelieve it, and a witness of the children of Israel has already testified to the like thereof and has believed, and you are too proud to accept. Lo! Allah will not guide wrong doing folk".).* And to show the closeness of his belief to that of the Israelites and the Christians we provide the following excerpts *(Surah 4: 136: "O you who believe! Believe in Allah and His messenger and the Scripture, which He has revealed unto His messenger, and the Scripture, which He revealed beforehand. Who disbelieves in Allah and His angels and His scriptures and His messengers and the Last Day, he verily has wandered far astray."*). Also, in *(Surah 2: 62: "Lo! Those who believe in that which is revealed unto you, Muhammad, and those who are Jews, and Christians, and Sabaeans who believe in Allah and the Last Day and does right – surely their reward is with their Lord, and there shall no fear come upon them neither shall they grieve.").* This last Surah is repeated in (Surah 5: 69).

The revelations in Mecca also requested Muslims not to argue with the People of the Scripture as per *(Surah 29: 46: "And argue not with the People of the Scripture but in the best way, save with such of them who do wrong, and say: We believe in that which has been revealed unto us and revealed unto you. Our God and your God is One, and unto him we surrender.").* We even find a stronger request from God to Muhammad in *(Surah 6: 52: "Repel not those who call upon their Lord at morn and evening, seeking His Countenance. You are not accountable for them in aught, nor are they accountable for you in aught, that you should repel them and be of the wrong doers.").* Those referred to here are Christian monks and Jewish Rabbis.

And to show the close ties between Muslims and the People of the Scripture, we read in *(Surah 5: 5: "This day are good things made lawful to you. The food of those who have received the Scripture is lawful for you, and your food is lawful for them. And so are the virtuous women of the believers and the virtuous women of those who received the Scripture before you lawful for you when you give them their marriage portions and live with them in honour, not in fornication, nor taking them as secret concubines.")*

Prophet Muhammad later tried to show the people of the Scripture that the true faith was distorted by some of their Rabbis and Christian clergy, and that only the Scripture revealed to him is to be followed as per *(Surah 5: 15: "O People of the Scripture! Now has Our messenger come unto you, expounding unto you much of that which you used to hide in the Scripture, and forgiving much. Now has come unto you light from Allah and a plain Scripture.").* Also in *(Surah 42: 14–15: "And they were not divided until after the knowledge came unto them, through rivalry among themselves… Therefore 'you Muhammad'… be upright as you are commanded… and say: I am commanded to be just among you. Allah is our Lord and your Lord. Unto us our works and unto you your works. No argument between you and us. Allah will bring us together, and unto Him is the journeying.").*

After the People of the Scripture's rejection to rally to his call, the following surah was revealed to Prophet Muhammad: (*Surah 3: 110: "You Muslims are the best community that has been raised up for mankind. You enjoin right conduct and forbid indecency, and you believe in Allah. And if the People of the Scripture had believed, it had been better for them. Some of them are believers, but most are evil-livers."*). And (*Surah 5: 48: "And unto you have We revealed the Scripture with the truth, confirming whatever Scripture was before it, and a watcher over it. So judge between them by that which Allah has revealed, and follow not their desires away from the truth, which has come unto you. For each, We have appointed a divine law and a traced-out way. Had Allah willed He could have made you one community but that He may try you by that which He has given you. So vie with one with another in good works. Unto Allah you will all return, and He will then inform you of that wherein you differ."*).

*

Later in Medina, after facing problems from the Jewish Rabbis came (*Surah 2: 109: "Many of the People of the Scripture long to make you disbelievers after your belief, through envy on their own account, after the truth has become manifest to them. Forgive and be indulgent until Allah give command."*).

At the end, when the situation between the local Jewish population of Yathrib (Medina) and the migrant Muslims who came with Muhammad from Mecca, and found refuge living among them worsened, and the Jews requested the departure of the migrants, and the payment of interest on loaned money to Muslims, the following was revealed to Muhammad: *(Surah 5: 51:* **"O you who believe! Take not the Jews and the Christians for friends. They are friends one to another. He** *amongst you who takes them for friends is one of them. Lo! Allah guides not wrongdoing folk.").* He was then commanded by Allah to fight the Jews in their towns: Yathrib, Kheibar and Fadak and to expel them out of their homes and towns as per *(Surah 5: 2:* **"He it is Who has caused those of the People of the Scripture who disbelieved to go forth from their homes unto the first exile...** *But Allah reached them from a place whereof they reckoned not...").*

Some Arab historians relate the origin of the tribe of Quraysh to Ishmael, the son of Abraham from his Egyptian slave woman Hagar, that according to the Bible – the Old Testament, Prophet Abraham deported to a faraway place in the desert out of jealousy of his wife Sarah (Genesis 21: 14–21). The sons of Ishmael married woman from the surrounding Arab and Midianite tribes (as did later Moses who married a Midianite woman, Exodus 16: 21). Prophet Muhammad in his call for the worship of a single God, relied on the Ishmaelite origin of his tribe, trying at the beginning to enlist the sympathy of the Jewish population of Yathrib and other cities of the Hejaz, who at the start of his peaceful call, showed him their support *(Surah 46: 10: "Say: Consider if it is (the Koran) from Allah and you disbelieve it, and a witness of the children of Israel has already testified to the like thereof and has believed, and you are too proud to accept. Lo! Allah will not guide wrong doing folk".),* basing his call on the common origin of the two branches of Abraham's lineage: Israelite and Ishmaelite, reiterating that he is the prophet they waited for in the Torah and the last of a long series of prophets. We can show his desire at the start of his call to cooperate with Jews and Christians, as we already have done in clause D3 above, and in many other Surah of the Koran (Surah 2: 62) (Surah 3: 84) (Surah 4: 136) and others.

At the beginning, the Jews of Yathrib sympathized with Muhammad who was calling his Arab fellows for the worship of a single God, the God of the Israelite prophets and the Torah, who faced in prayer (Qibla) the direction of Jerusalem as they did themselves. But after his victorious battles against the Arab pagans, and after he started his legislation (the Sharia) for the establishment of a new Arab state based on divine revelations to his person, and also his refusal to pay them interest on money they loaned him and his companions, his talk about Jesus son of Mary – the Messiah who came and was persecuted by the children of Israel as per *(Surah 3: 55: "When Allah said: O Jesus! Lo! I am allowing your death and taking you up to me and cleansing you of those who disbelieve and I am setting those who follow you above those who disbelieve until the Day of Resurrection...")*, and (Surah 61: 14: *"... even as Jesus son of Mary said to his disciples: Who are my helpers for Allah? They said: we are Allah's helpers. And a party of the Children of Israel believed, while a party disbelieved. Then, we strengthened those who believed against their foe, and they became the uppermost.")*, and his change of the Qibla from Jerusalem to Al-Kaaba in Mecca, as per (Surah 2: 144), the relations between the two sides worsened.

The above reasons caused a divine revelation commanding him not to trust them but to fight them as per *(Surah 5: 82: "You will find the most vehement of mankind in hostility to those who believe to be the Jews and the idolaters. And you will find the nearest in affection to those who believe those who say: Lo! We are Christians. That is because there are among them priests and monks, and because they are not proud.")*. Thereafter, he waged war against the Jewish tribes of Kainaka' and Bani-Nadir in Yathrib, wars that ended with their expulsion from the city, allowing them to take away whatever they could carry on their camel backs. Their houses, land and other assets were made personal property of Prophet Muhammad (Imam Al-Balaziri – *the Countries*

Conquests – Part 1 *The wealth of Bani Nadir* "... The messenger of God besieged them 15 nights. At its end they reconciled him by agreeing to leave the city, taking with them only what their camels could carry, leaving behind them their weapons, furniture, livestock, houses, land and crops. All their wealth became sole property of the messenger of God"). After their expulsion from Yathrib, he waged war on other Jewish tribes who lived in the nearby cities of Khaibar and the oasis of Fadak, and expulsed them leaving behind all their property, thereby all their wealth became the personal property of the Prophet. The final expulsion of all Jews from Hejaz was carried out by Caliph Omar Ibn Al-Khattab (Al-Balaziri – *the Countries Conquests*).

It was not surprising that after Prophet Muhammad subjected Mecca to his rule, he has extended it over the pagan Arab tribes in the Hejaz and the Arabian Peninsula, and expelled the Jewish tribes from the Hejaz cities, that the turn of the Christian populations of Arabia and the countries at its periphery should come. The following command from Allah was now revealed to Prophet Muhammad *(Surah 9: 29-30:* **"Fight against such of those who have been given the Scripture as believe not in Allah nor the Last Day,** *and forbid not that which Allah and His messenger has forbidden , and follow not the Religion of Truth, until they pay the tribute readily, being brought low... Allah himself fought against them. How perverse are they.")*

6. D 4 Fight against the idolaters and disbelievers

The Koran's account resembles that of the Torah but with one major difference: The enemy here is an enemy who does not believe in Allah nor in his messenger Muhammad, while the enemy in the Torah was an ethnic one: the nations residing in the Land of Canaan.

Therefore Allah in the Koran demands to fight the idolaters and the disbelievers as per *(Surah 2: 191: "And slay them wherever you find them, and drive them out of the places whence they drove you out, for incitement is worse than slaughter…")* and in *(Surah 2: 193: "And fight them until persecution is no more, and religion is for Allah…")* and in *(Surah 2: 216: "Warfare is ordained for you, though it is hateful unto you…")* and in *(Surah 2: 244: "Fight in the way of Allah, and know that Allah is Hearer, Knower")* and in *(Surah 4: 74: "Let those fight in the way of Allah who sell the life of this world for the other. Who fights in the way of Allah, be he slain or be he victorious, on him We shall bestow a vast reward")* and *in (Surah 4: 89: "… if they turn back to enmity then take them and kill them wherever you find them, and choose no friend nor helper among them")* and in *(Surah 4: 91: "… If they keep not aloof from you… then take them and kill them wherever you find them…")* and in *(Surah 5: 33: "The only reward of those who make war upon Allah and His messenger… will be that they will be killed or crucified, or have their hands and feet on alternate sides cut off, or will be expelled out of the land.")* and in *(Surah 9: 12: "And if they break their pledge after their treaty and assail your religion, then fight the heads of disbelief…")* and in *(Surah 47: 4: "Now when you meet those who disbelieve, then smite of their necks until, when you have routed them, then fasten them with bonds…")*, and many others. We should add here that Allah requests Muslims after having fought, killed and/or captured their enemies to let the captives free if they repent, in certain surahs as in *(Surah 9: 5: "Then, when the sacred months have passed, slay the idolaters whenever you find them, and take them captive, and besiege them, and prepare for them each ambush. But if they repent and establish worship and pay the poor-due, then leave their way free...")*, and Surah 2: 193 and certain others.

We find also Allah demanding to terrorize the enemy as in *(Surah 8: 60: "Make ready for them all you can of armed forces and of tethered horses, that thereby you may terrorize the enemy of Allah and your enemy...")* and demanding Prophet Muhammad to incite the believers to fight as *in (Surah 8: 65–67: "O Prophet! Exhort the believers to fight. If there be of you twenty steadfast they shall overcome two hundred... It is not for any prophet to have captives until he has made slaughter in the land...")*.

Also Allah made it lawful for believers to take war booty as per *(Surah 8: 69: "Now enjoy the booty you have taken as lawful and keep your duty to Allah. Lo! Allah is forgiving, Merciful.")*, and *(Surah 48: 20: "Allah promised you much booty that you will capture, and has given you this in advance, and has withheld men's hands from you, that it may be a token for the believers, and that He may guide you on a right path.")*.

The reaction of Prophet Muhammad to his maltreatment by Quraysh – his tribe, was somewhat similar to that of the kings of Israel, as he was commanded to fight the idolaters and disbelievers until his victorious entry to Mecca.

After Prophet Muhammad's victories on the idolaters of Mecca and Arabia and the expulsion of the Jewish tribes from the cities of Yathrib, Kheibar and Fadak, he felt the need to direct the fighting energies of the nomadic Arab tribes of the Arabian Peninsula, who were superficially Islamized, to an external enemy in order to preserve the unity of the new Muslim nation state he has just created and to prevent infighting. Accordingly, he directed a Muslim army towards the towns of Tabuk, Eilat, Ezrah and Maqna – towns located in southern Syria and inhabited by Christians, who according to *(Surah 5: 82 were: "the nearest in affection to those who believe")*, who didn't commit any aggressive act against the prophet and his companions, basing his war effort on a new revelation *(Surah 9: 29: "Fight against such of those who have been given the Scripture as believe not in Allah nor the Last Day, and forbid not that which Allah and His messenger has forbidden, and follow not the Religion of Truth, until they pay the tribute readily, being brought low...").* And *(Surah 5: 48: "And unto you have We revealed the Scripture with the truth, confirming whatever Scripture was before it, **and a watcher over it**. So judge between them by that which Allah has revealed, and follow not their desires away from the truth which has come unto you...")*

After these revelations, not only the Jews had to be fought but also the Christians, as now it appeared that they have misinterpreted the Scriptures, and it was the duty of Prophet Muhammad to lead them to the true religion – Islam, by force if required, or by payment of tribute, as directed and requested by Allah.

※

To summarize: The spread of the new faith (Islam) occurred fighting the idolaters (battles of Badr, Uhod, Al-Khandaq), then the Jews in the Hejaz cities that ended with their expulsion, then fighting the rebellion of Arab tribes during the life of Prophet Muhammad as well as after his death, and finally fighting against the Christian East Roman Empire of Byzantium and the Persian Sassanid Empire (battles of Ajnadin, Yarmouk, Zee-Kar and Al-Qadisyah...) in Syria, Iraq, Egypt, Persia and North Africa.

The new Muslim faith was spread through wars of conquest conducted in the early years, by Prophet Muhammad and his companions, but mostly by religiously ignorant nomadic Arabs who rode the wave of the victorious Islam, as it became their lawful tool to spoils of war, as per (*Surah 48: 16: "Say to those of the wandering Arabs who were left behind: You will be called against a people of mighty prowess, to fight them until they surrender; and if you obey, Allah will give you a fair reward...*), as most of Muhammad's companions (the Koran readers) died during the war against the apostasy (ridda) of the tribe of Banu Hanifa headed by Musailima that rose against the rule of the first caliph Abu Bakr after the death of Prophet Muhammad. These wars of conquest under the banner of the new religion (Islam) represented for the poor and hungry nomad Arabs a way of wresting tribute and enriching themselves at the expense of the settled and opulent subdued peoples. Printing techniques during the seventh century AD were not known and people capable of reading and writing were counted on the single hand's fingers. The best that the third Caliph Othman Bin Affan was able to do after twenty-two years of Prophet Muhammad's death, was to assemble with the greatest difficulty three hand copies of the Koran, one sent to Damascus, the other to Kufa in Iraq, the third copy he kept to himself in Medina.

Most of the fighters of the Arab armies were nomads who had a faint idea about Islam. They were illiterate unable to read the Koran. The same applied to the non-Arab conquered peoples of Syria, Mesopotamia, Egypt, Persia and North Africa who didn't speak Arabic. Repeating the words of: "No God but Allah and Muhammad is his Messenger" in Arabic, without even understanding the full meaning of these words, was enough for any foreign defeated person to become Muslim, and in so doing avoid being killed or enslaved with payment of tribute. Many poor Christians unable to pay the tribute and the majority of pagan Persian and Berber (Amazigh) populations of North Africa converted to Islam in this manner as a result of the Arab Islamic conquests. The Rashidun caliphs and later the Omayyad and Abbasid caliphs as well as the Ottoman Sultans followed the rules established by Prophet Muhammad in his dealings with the Jews of Yathrib, Khaibar and Fadak and the Christians of Najran, Eilat, Azrah and Mukna, as reported by Al-Yakoubi in his fourth volume and Imam Al-Balaziri's book: *The Countries Conquests* – Part 1.

These rules translated into payment of tribute by the non-fighting vanquished 'Peoples of the Scripture' if they do not convert to Islam, as per (Surah 9: 29). The policy of tribute payment was extended and applied also onto the defeated Zoroastrian Persian and pagan Berber populations. In case of resistance, men were killed, all their property taken as spoils of war, young boys and girls as well as women were sold in slave markets. The trade in slaves, especially beautiful girls and boys was widely spread during the period of Muslim Arab Caliphates and later, Turkish Sultanates, when caliphs, sultans and lesser governors kept large harems comprising big numbers of slave women and eunuchs.

Recently, during years 2013–18, the Islamic State in Iraq and Syria (ISIS) thought to apply the practices of Prophet Muhammad and his Companions "the Good Salaf" by imposing tribute on the Christian populations of Syria and Iraq if they submit, killing Yazidi and Alawite men (disbelievers – Kafirs) and enslaving/plundering their women and children.

6. E. Comparison between the Koran's Sharia Law and Moses' Law

6. E. 1. Food and Clothing:

There is a striking similarity between the Sharia Law and Moses' Law in respect to unlawful food, as there is much resemblance between the Koran's *(Surah 5: 3: "Forbidden unto you are carrion and blood and swine flesh, and that has been dedicated unto other than Allah, and the strangled, and the dead through beating... and the devoured of wild beasts...")* and the Old *Testament's (Leviticus 11: 1-41: "And the Lord spoke to Moses and Aaron, saying to them, ... These are the living things that you may eat among all the animals that are on the earth. Whatever parts the hoof and is cloven-footed and chews the cud, among the animals, you may eat. Nevertheless you shall not eat these: The camel, because it chews the cud but does not part the hoof... And the hare... and the pig."*

"These you may eat, of all that are in the waters. Everything in the waters that has fins and scales, whether in the seas or in the rivers, you may eat.... And these you shall detest among the birds, they shall not be eaten: the eagle, the vulture, the kite, the falcon of any kind, every raven of any kind, the ostrich, the seagull, the hawk of any kind, the little owl, the cormorant and others."

"All winged insects that go on all fours are detestable to you. Yet among the winged insects that go on all fours you may eat those that have jointed legs above their feet, with which to hop on the ground. Of them you may eat: the locust of any kind... And these are unclean to you among the swarming things that swarm on the ground: the mole rat, the mouse, the great lizard of any kind, the gecko, the monitor lizard, the lizard, the sand lizard, and the chameleon. And if any animal which you may eat dies, whoever touches its carcass shall be unclean until the evening, and whoever eats of its carcass shall wash his clothes and be unclean until the evening")

And to (Leviticus 17: 10: "If any one of the house of Israel or of the strangers who sojourn among them eats any blood, I will set my face against that person who eats blood and will cut him off from among his people.") and *(*Deuteronomy 12: 16: "Only you shall not eat the blood; you shall pour it out on the earth like water."), and (Deuteronomy 14: 21: "You shall not eat anything that has died naturally. You may give it to the sojourner who is within your towns, that he may eat it, or you may sell it to a foreigner. For you are a people holy to the LORD your God."), and (Deuteronomy 32: 35–38: "Vengeance is mine, and recompense, for the time when their foot shall slip; ….Where are their gods, the rock in which they took refuge, who ate the fat of their sacrifices and drank the wine of their drink offering?").

The similarity between what was lawfully permitted for food consumption between the Koran and the Torah is made clear from *(Surah 5: 5: "This day are good things made lawful for you. The food of those who have received the Scripture is lawful for you, and your food is lawful for them…").* The People of the Scripture referred to here were the Jews and the Nazarene (as we mentioned above, they were Christians who followed Moses' Law).

It is beneficial here to remind the reader that the peoples of the Ancient Near East including the Akkadians, Babylonians, Assyrians, Amorites, Arameans and Egyptians considered pork to be an unclean animal (as reported in Herodotus Book two) and were prohibited to eat its flesh, so the request to avoid eating it in the Old Testament and Koran were just a confirmation of what was an old Near Eastern tradition.

Regarding camel and some other animal's flesh, prohibited in Moses' Law, the Koran made their consumption lawful based on what Jesus in the Koran said *(Surah 3: 50: "… and to make lawful some of that which was forbidden unto you…").*

Wine was not forbidden in the Old or the New Testament, nor in the Koran. In the Koran, Muslims were requested not to pray while drunk and not to over consume it, as its harm exceeds its benefits. In the Old Testament we find in (Leviticus 10: 9: "Drink no wine or strong drink, you or your sons with you, when you go into the tent of meeting, lest you die. It shall be a statute forever throughout your generations.") and in (Numbers 6: 2: "Speak to the people of Israel and say to them, When either a man or a woman makes a special vow, the vow of a Nazirite, to separate himself to the Lord, he shall separate himself from wine and strong drink").

In the Koran, we find a similar attitude towards alcoholic drinks. In *(Surah 16: 67: "And of the fruits of the date palm, and grapes, whence you derive strong drink and also good nourishment...")*, and in *(Surah 2: 219: "They question you about strong drink and games of chance. Say: in both is great sin and utility for men. But the sin of them is greater than their usefulness...")*, and in *(Surah 4: 43: "O you who believe! Draw not near unto prayer when you are drunken, till you know that which you utter...")*, and *in (Surah 5: 90: "O you who believe! Strong drink and games of chance and idols and divining arrows are only an infamy of Satan's handiwork. Leave it aside in order that you may succeed").*

This last Surah is crystal clear as it requested believers to leave strong drink aside, but not prohibiting strong drinks, and the difference between the prohibited (Haram) and the set aside is quite big, and how could wine and strong drinks be prohibited by God if there are flowing rivers of wine in Paradise? As per *(Surah 47: 15: "A similitude of the Garden which those who keep their duty to Allah are promised: therein are rivers of water unpolluted, and rivers of milk whereof the flavour changes not, and rivers of wine delicious to the drinkers...").*

On this subject we must quote the Muslim historian Ibn Khaldoun in his book: The *Introduction, Part 1*, page 20, saying "... the attitude of Caliph Haroun Al-Rashid in avoiding wine drinking was well known to his courtiers... Al-Rashid drank palm's fermented juice (Nabiz) according to the habits of the Iraqis, and their fatwas in wine drinking were well known".

Regarding clothing rules, we read in the Old Testament (Deuteronomy 22: 5: "A woman shall not wear a man's garment, nor shall a man put on a woman's cloak, for whoever does these things is an abomination to the Lord your God"). And in (Leviticus 19: 27: "You shall not round off the hair on your temples or mar the edges of your beard").

It is interesting here to note that this prohibition didn't include shaving the moustache. Many Muslims nowadays shave their moustache to emulate Prophet Muhammad and some Jewish Rabbis.

Talmudic instructions requested women to put on decent clothing that does not show their naked bodies and to cover their head's hair. Also, it requested the faithful not to disfigure their bodies as per (Leviticus 19: 28: "You shall not make any cuts on your body for the dead or tattoo yourselves: I am the Lord"). As we already know, God requested from Abraham to circumcise male children as in (Genesis 17: 12–13: "He who is eight days old among you shall be circumcised. Every male throughout your generations, whether born in your house or bought with your money from any foreigner who is not of your offspring, both he who is born in your house and he who is bought with your money, shall surely be circumcised. So shall my covenant be in your flesh an everlasting covenant.").

Circumcision of male children cannot be found in the Koran, it is not mentioned in the New Testament either. This practice is very old and was widespread in Ancient Egypt and in Ethiopia (Herodotus in his *Histories* Book 2 wrote: "They practice circumcision, while men of other nations – except those who have learned from Egypt, leave their private parts as nature made them"), and from there it spread to the Hebrews and some Arab tribes.

Regarding clothing habits in the Ancient Near East, and due to the location of these countries in a hot and dry climate close to deserts, it was natural for the local populations to cover their heads to protect themselves from the hot sunrays and dust. We read in (Herodotus, the *Histories* Book 2: "The priests shave their heads... They shave their bodies all over every other day to guard against the presence of lice... they cover their heads to protect them from the sun..."). The habit of covering men's heads is still widespread nowadays in many countries of the Near East, as in Egypt, Saudi Arabia, the Persian Gulf Arab countries, Iraq, Jordan and others. Women of the Ancient Near East also covered their heads, to protect their long hair from dust, as apart from Egypt, water was a scarce resource. Due to the rarity of trees and woodlands to provide peoples of this region with a feeling of privacy, unlike the populations of surrounding countries of Asia Minor and Europe, women dressed from ancient times with flowing robes and long sleeves, as are depicted the "veiled" women of Palmyra", on stone carvings dating from the first century AD. The same tradition is expressed in the icons of the Virgin Mary, where she is shown always with a head scarf, and the dress of the Christian nuns. Islam came to confirm these eastern dress traditions that contrasted the way of life of the Greek and Roman settlers in Syria, Palestine and Egypt, where women (and men) didn't cover their heads and some other parts of their bodies. That's the essence of *(Surah 33: 59: "O Prophet! Tell your wives and your daughters and the women of the believers to draw their cloaks close round them. That will be better, so that they may be recognized and not annoyed."),* and *(Surah 24: 31: "And tell to the believing women to lower their gaze and guard their private parts and to display of their adornment only that which is apparent, and to draw their veils over their bosoms...").* These old eastern dressing traditions are on display nowadays in most Muslim countries (and lately, in some European countries as well).

6. E. 2. Women in Islam:

a. Marriage:

Marriage with more than one woman was widespread among the Israelites as well as among the pagan Arabs before Islam, but that was not the case among Christians and the Arab Christian Nazarene. This fact might possibly explain why Prophet Muhammad didn't marry more than his first wife Khadija till her death at age 65, (he was then about 50 years old) as she was probably a Christian Nazarene (Christian priest Waraqa Ibn Naoufal was her uncle), besides the respect he felt for her as she was a woman of great wealth, strong personality, great ethics and social standing.

Christians based their belief in marrying not more than one woman on The Old Testament, (Genesis 2: 21-24: "the Lord God caused a deep sleep to fall upon the man, and while he slept took one of his ribs and closed up its place with flesh. And the rib that the Lord God had taken from the man he made into a woman and brought her to the man... Therefore a man shall leave his father and his mother and hold fast to his wife, and they shall become one flesh."), where God created only one woman: Eve to Adam, and also on Jesus Christ's answer to the Pharisees (Mathew 19: 4–6: "He answered, have you not read that He who created them from the beginning made them male and female, and said, 'Therefore a man shall leave his father and his mother and hold fast to his wife, and the two shall become one flesh... What therefore God has joined together, let not man separate.").

In spite of God's command to the kings of Israel not to marry many women: (Deuteronomy 17: 17–19: "And he shall not acquire many wives for himself, lest his heart turn away, nor shall he acquire for himself excessive silver and gold. And when he sits on the throne of his kingdom, he shall write for himself in a book a copy of this law, approved by the Levitical priests. And it shall be with him, and he shall read in it all the days of his life, that he may learn to fear the Lord his God"). The Israelite prophets and kings married many women. We find Prophet Muhammad following their example, keeping eleven wives after his immigration to Yathrib, making considerable efforts to write and recite the old scriptures and Allah's revelations during his lifetime, as commanded above by God in the Torah.

In the Koran, we read in *(Surah 4: 3: "And if you fear that you will not deal fairly with the orphans, marry of the women, who seem good to you, two or three or four, and if you fear that you cannot do justice to so many, then one only, or the captive women that your right hands possess.")*.

Also *in (Surah 4: 129: "You will not be able to deal equally between your wives, however much you wish to do so. But turn not altogether away leaving her in suspense.")*. In this last surah, God makes it clear that no man can deal justly between many wives, and that the resolution of the problem could be difficult (could divorce be the solution?).

Many Muslim Oulema (doctors in Law) and scholars do not base their interpretation on this last surah (Surah 4: 129) but interpret it in a way that satisfies their instincts, basing their interpretation on (Surah 4: 3) and the example of Prophet Muhammad who married many women besides the women his right hand possessed (captive women – spoils of war against the enemies of Allah), not taking into consideration that Prophet Muhammad was exempt from the ruling Allah imposed on all Muslim men as per *(Surah 33: 50: "O Prophet! Lo! We have made lawful unto you your wives unto whom you has paid their dowries, and those women whom your right hand possessed of those whom Allah has given you as spoils of war, and the daughters of your uncles on the father's side and the daughters of your aunts on the father's side, and the daughters of your uncles on the mother's side, and the daughters of your aunts on the mother's side who emigrated with you, and a believing woman if she gives herself unto the Prophet and the Prophet desires to marry her – a privilege for you only, not for the rest of the believers. We are aware of that which We enjoined upon them concerning their wives and those whom their right hands possess – that you may be free from blame."*).

Also on *(Surah 33: 37: "And when you said unto him on whom Allah has conferred favour and you has conferred favour: keep your wife to yourself, and fear Allah. And you did hide in your mind that which Allah was to bring to light, and you did fear mankind whereas Allah has a better right that you should fear him. So when Zeyd had performed the necessary formality from her, we gave her unto you in marriage…"*). Here Allah allowed the marriage of Prophet Muhammad with the wife of his adopted son Zeyd: Zeinab Bint Jahch, after Zeyd had to divorce her, due to the Prophet's desire to marry her.

The above Koran revelations therefore made it clear that Allah exempted Prophet Muhammad from what He made unlawful to all other humans, and therefore Prophet Muhammad shall not be an example to follow by men in many respects.

As we made it clear in Chapter 6 Clause C, Allah's revelations to Prophet Muhammad took place during more than twenty years. During that period of time, the status of Prophet Muhammad evolved becoming that of a leading statesman, so that the "revelations" had to take account of the changing geopolitical and social scenery including those related to the changing status, perception and thinking of Prophet Muhammad himself – the tool of the "revelations". The above mentioned (Surah 4: 129) very clearly states that marrying more than one woman could lead only to injustice, and such injustice will be punished by Allah.

*

Prophet Muhammad having been allowed (Surah 33: 50) to marry eleven women (1. Khadija, 2. Saouda, 3. Aycha, 4. Hafsa, 5. Zaynab Bint Khuzaima, 6. Um Salma, 7. Zaynab Bint Jahsh (ex-wife of his adopted son Zaid), 8. Jourieh, 9. Um Habiba, 10. Safia the Jewish, 11. Maimouneh) besides the captive plundered women, was accused by most of his wives of dealing unfairly and unequally between them. The squabbles and fights between the Prophet and his wives Aysha, Hafsa, Zaynab and his other wives are well known and documented in the Correct Al-Hadith. These fights provoked Allah to interfere on his behalf and threaten the Prophet's wives with *divorce (Surah 66: 5: "It may happen that his Lord, if he divorce you, will give him in your stead wives better than you, submissive, believing, pious, penitent, devout, inclined to fasting, … and virgins.")*. Allah also absolved the Prophet from the oath given to his wife Hafsa as in *(Surah 66: 1–2: "O Prophet! Why are you banishing that which Allah has made lawful for you, seeking to please your wives?... Allah has made lawful for you absolution from your oaths and Allah is your protector...")*,

Allah confirming again that Prophet Muhammad is exempt from His commandments to all other humans.

It follows from the above revelations that Prophet Muhammad should not be an example to be followed by men, as he was exempt from most of God's rules and regulations.

*

The Koran forbade the marriage of relatives as in *(Surah 4: 23: "Forbidden unto you are your mothers, and your daughters, and your sisters, and your father's sisters, and your mother's sisters and your brother's daughters, and your sister's daughters, and your foster mothers, and your foster sisters, and your mothers-in-law,...")*. This is similar to what we find in the Old Testament, (Leviticus 18: 6–20: "None of you shall approach any one of his close relatives to uncover nakedness. I am the Lord. You shall not uncover the nakedness of your father... and your mother. You shall not uncover the nakedness of your father's wife... of your sister, your father's daughter or your mother's daughter... of your son's daughter or of your daughter's daughter, ... of your father's wife's daughter, ... of your father's sister... of your mother's sister... of your father's brother's wife... of your daughter-in-law... of your brother's wife... And you shall not take a woman as a rival wife to her sister, while her sister is still alive. You shall not approach a woman to uncover her nakedness while she is in her menstrual uncleanness. And you shall not lie sexually with your neighbour's wife and so make yourself unclean with her"). And (Leviticus 18: 22–23: "You shall not lie with a male as with a woman; it is an abomination. And you shall not lie with any animal and so make yourself unclean with it, neither shall any woman give herself to an animal to lie with it: it is perversion.").

b. *Divorce:*

We find in the Old Testament (Deuteronomy 2:, 1–4: "When a man takes a wife and marries her, if then she finds no favour in his eyes because he has found some indecency in her, and he writes her a certificate of divorce and puts it in her hand and sends her out of his house, and she departs out of his house... ").

The status of women in the Torah is much inferior to that of men. Men had the right to divorce their wives for a cause and without a cause and women did not. Recently, Jewish Rabbis awoke to this injustice and are making it a condition for divorce to be valid that the women should give their consent.

In Islam, divorce is more difficult, as the Koran demands that men repeat the words: "You are divorced," twice before consuming the divorce *(Surah 2: 229: "Divorce must be pronounced twice and then a woman must be retained in honour or released in kindness...").* To make divorce even more difficult, it places as a condition that the woman shall wed another man before she can return to her previous husband *(Surah 2; 230: "And if he has divorced her, then she is not lawful to him thereafter until she has wedded another husband. Then if the other husband divorces her, it is no sin for both of them that they come together again...").* This last verse contradicts the Torah, as per (Deuteronomy 24: 1–4: "her former husband, who sent her away, may not take her again to be his wife, after she has been defiled, for that is an abomination before the Lord.").

The status of women in the Koran is a degree lower than men and was made clear *from (Surah 4: 34: "Men are in charge of women, because Allah has made the one of them to excel the other, and because they spend of their money for their support... As for those women from whom you fear rebellion, admonish them and banish them to beds apart, and beat (scourge) them. Then, if they obey you, seek not a way against them.").*

It is worth mentioning that Allah preferred men over women in many verses of the Koran, as in *(Surah 2: 228: "Women... and men are a degree above them, Allah is Mighty, Wise."), and (Surah 43, 16: "Or did He chose daughters of all that He has created and He honoured you with sons?"),* and *(Surah 43: 19: "And they make the angels, who are the slaves of the Beneficent, females...")* and *(Surah 16: 57: "And they assign into Allah daughters – Be He glorified!, and unto themselves what they desire."), and many other verses.*

c.   *Litigation and inheritance:*
We read in *(Surah 4: 11: "Allah charged you concerning your children: to the male the equivalent of the portion of two females..."), and we read on what concerns litigation in (Surah 2: 282: "... And call to witness, from among your men, two witnesses. And if two men are not at hand then a man and two women, of such as you approve as witnesses, so that if the one erred through forgetfulness, the other will remember...").*

*

To summarize regarding the status of women in Islam, we can say that it was better than what was their fate in pagan and tribal Arabia and possibly also in the Torah, but inferior to what was their status in nearby Christian countries, where Christianity gave women a respected position in the family and society.

Marriage in Christianity is considered a mystery as God in the beginning created one woman: Eva to Adam the first man. That's why, Christianity forbade polygamy. Regarding divorce, we read in (Matthew 19: 7–9: "They said to him, why then did Moses command one to give a certificate of divorce and to send her away? He said to them: Because of your hardness of heart Moses allowed you to divorce your wives, but from the beginning it was not so. And I say to you: whoever divorces his wife, except for sexual immorality, and marries another, commits adultery".).

Christian Churches allow divorce only in case of adultery. Apart from this case, the Church might agree in rare cases to the dissolution of marriage, after allowing enough time to heal any bad feelings, and if all rapprochement between the couple fails, and make it very difficult in case the couple has children. Jesus Christ proclaimed husband and wife united in a single body, with no distinction of one over the other whatsoever, both of them equal in rights and duties before God.

6. E. 3. Prayers, Ablutions and Fasting:

a. Direction of prayer – the Qibla

We read in the Torah *(1 Kings : 44: "If your people go out to battle against their enemy, by whatever way you shall send them, and they pray to the Lord toward the city that you have chosen and the house that I have built for your name, then hear in heaven their prayer and their plea, and maintain their cause.")*, which meant that the Israelites prayed facing the Solomon's Temple in Jerusalem. As we already mentioned above, Prophet Muhammad and his companions prayed initially facing the direction of Solomon's Temple in Jerusalem (the temple was then in ruins after Titus destroyed it in AD 70), which was the first Muslim Qibla (Masjid Al-Aqsa – the first Muslim Qibla mentioned in the Koran, (Surah 17: 1) didn't exist in Muhammad's days. The present-day Masjid Al-Aqsa was built about 59 years after the death of Prophet Muhammad by the Omayad Caliph Abdel Malek in AD 691).

Later, after enmity broke out between the Muslims and the Jewish population of Yathrib, and in an effort to reconcile his tribe Quraysh whose pagan shrine – the Kaaba in Mecca was a source of income as a religious and trade centre, Allah allowed to Prophet Muhammad to turn while praying towards the Kaaba in Mecca (Surah 2: 144), and made it his new Qibla instead of Jerusalem.

No mention in the Koran about the exact number of daily prayers and their exact timing, apart from that mentioned in *(Surah 30: 17–18: "So glory be to Allah when you enter the night and you enter the morning. Unto him be praise in the heavens and the earth! And at the sun's decline and the noonday.")*, amounting to four prayers, and *(Surah 2: 238: "Be guardians of your prayers, and of the midmost prayer...")* which could be interpreted as being the middle one of any odd number: 3, 5, etc...

Muslims after the death of the Prophet couldn't agree on which prayer was meant to be the "midmost" prayer. Only under the Abbasid Caliphs, did they settle on five prayers, possibly using the five daily divisions and prayers of the day from the Ancient Zoroastrian Religion.

Accordingly, Jews turn to Jerusalem during prayers and Muslims toward Mecca. As for Christians, they don't have to pray in a certain direction, as they believe God who exists everywhere will accept it in whichever direction they pray.

b. **Ablutions**

We read in the Torah *(*Exodus 30: 20–21: "When they go into the tent of meeting, or when they come near the altar to minister... They shall wash their hands and their feet, so that they may not die. It shall be a statute forever to them, even to him and to his offspring throughout their generations."), and in the Koran, *(Surah 5: 6: "O you who believe, When you rise up for prayer, wash your faces, and your hands up to the elbows, and lightly rub your heads and wash your feet up to the ankles...")*, which is nearly what the Jews do before prayers. This habit and others was probably borrowed from the Jewish Rabbis of Yathrib.

c. **Fasting**

We read in the Torah (Exodus 34: 28: "So he was there with the Lord forty days and forty nights. He neither ate bread nor drank water. And he wrote on the tablets the words of the covenant, the Ten Commandments".), and in *(*Leviticus 23: 27: "Now on the tenth day of this seventh month is the Day of Atonement. It shall be for you a time of holy convocation, and you shall afflict yourselves (fast) and present a food offering to the Lord"). In the Koran we read in (*Surah 2: 183: "O you who believe! Fasting is prescribed for you, even as it was prescribed for those before you, that you may ward off evil."*). Muslims observe the fast during the lunar month of Ramadan, during which the first surahs of the Koran were revealed in that cave close to Mecca to Muhammad. Muslims abstain from food and water during daylight hours.

6. E. 4. The Sharia Limits:

The Limits are penalties, inflicted for transgression against Allah's Law as per *(Surah 4: 14: "And who disobeys Allah and his Messenger and transgress His limits, He will make him enter Fire, where he will dwell for ever; his will be a shameful doom.").* Also *(Surah 65: 1: "… Such are the limits imposed by Allah; and who transgresses Allah's limits, he verily wrongs his soul.").*

Allah's limits include those for: Retaliation, theft, adultery, false witness/charge and apostasy.

*

The penalty for killing a Muslim is according to *(Surah 2: 178: "O you who believe! Retaliation is prescribed for you in the matter of the murdered; the freeman for the freeman, and the slave for the slave, and the female for the female…"),* and in *(Surah 5: 45: "And We prescribed for them therein: The life for the life, and the eye for the eye, and the nose for the nose, and the ear for the ear, and the tooth for the tooth,…").* The above much resembles the clauses of Moses' Law in the Old Testament, made two thousand years before Muhammad, requesting retaliation as in (Leviticus 24: 17–21: "Whoever takes a human life shall surely be put to death… If anyone injures his neighbour, as he has done it shall be done to him, fracture for fracture, eye for eye, tooth for tooth; whatever injury he has given a person shall be given to him…").

*

The penalty for theft is specified in *(Surah 5: 38–39: "As for the thief, both male and female, cut off their hands. It is the reward for their own deeds, an exemplary punishment from Allah. Allah is Mighty, Wise. But who repents after his wrongdoing and amends, lo! Allah will relent toward him. Allah is Forgiving, Merciful").* Here some Muslim scholars believe that repentance should be accepted by the religious tribunals before carrying out the amputation, while others make its acceptance very difficult by setting certain conditions.

*

The penalty for adultery is provided in *(Surah 24: 2: "The adulterer and the adulteress, scourge each of them with a hundred stripes (lashes). And let not pity for the twain withhold you from obedience to Allah... And let a party of believers witness their punishment.").* But for punishment to take place, the Koran placed as precondition: 1. that the adulterers should confess their act of their own accord, or 2. Four witnesses under oath shall confirm the act of adultery.

*

The stoning of adulterers cannot be found anywhere in the Koran, but the Sharia Doctors in Law base their decision for stoning the adulterers on the following *Correct Hadith* by Caliph Omar Ibn Al-Khatab: "Stoning of adulterers was revealed in the Koran; we read it and I can vouch for it. The Prophet himself stoned adulterers and we did follow his example after his death".

A similar testimony was made by other Companions of the Prophet, who confirmed its existence, but reported that it was later deleted when the Koran was gathered into a single book. The deletion of this Surah was reported in the *Correct Hadith* (speeches attributed to Prophet Muhammad) by Imam Al-Bukhary, Imam Muslim and attested by a number of other Muslim scholars.

*

The penalty for false witness is provided in *(Surah 24: 4: "And those who accuse honourable women but bring not four witnesses, scourge them with eighty stripes and never afterwards accept their testimony – They indeed are evildoers.")*. This Surah was revealed to Muhammad after his young wife Aisha (about nine years old when he married her) lost her way during the night and was brought back to camp by a young soldier the following day, after a battle fought against Bani Al-Mustaliq, pushing some bad tongues to talk about adultery.

*

As for wine drinking, no penalty was set for it in the Koran. The only mention of a punishment administered to a drunken man, reported in the *Correct Hadith,* was when Prophet Muhammad requested his companions to beat a drunken man and expel him from his presence. No consensus amongst Muslim Oulema and scholars exists about a penalty for wine drinking.

*

The same applies for apostasy, as no clear penalty was set for it in the Koran, apart from unspecified awful doom during life and Fire in the Hereafter. We read in *(Surah 3: 90: "Lo! Those who disbelieve after their profession of belief, and afterward grow violent in disbelief: their repentance will not be accepted.")*. Also *in (Surah 16: 106: "Who disbelieves in Allah after his belief... but who finds ease in disbelief: on him is wrath from Allah. Theirs will be an awful doom.")*, also in *(Surah 2: 217: "... And who becomes a renegade and dies in his disbelief: such are they whose works have fallen in the world and the Hereafter. Such are rightful owners of the Fire...")*.

Most Sunni Muslim scholars base their opinion on the penalty for apostasy on the *Correct Hadith*, as mentioned in (Sahih Al-Bukhari, 9-83-17) where Prophet Muhammad reportedly said: "Shedding the blood of a Muslim could be carried out only in three cases: adultery after abstinence, apostasy after confession of faith, or the killing of another Muslim". Also, it was reported by Imam Al-Bukhari and Imam Muslim that Prophet Muhammad said: "Kill any Muslim who rejects Islam".

Many Sunni Muslim scholars believe that there is no need for a clear Sharia limit to be found in the Koran, as the *Correct Hadith* and the Prophet's Sunna (example) complement the Koran. All these scholars agree on the principle that the renegade Muslim should be killed.

*

In the Torah, in Chapter 1 above, we mentioned the penalty for theft. In the Torah, the thief had to return two to five times the amount of the stolen items (Exodus 22: 1–4: "If a man steals an ox or a sheep, and kills it or sells it, he shall repay five oxen for an ox, and four sheep for a sheep. If a thief is found breaking in and is struck so that he dies, there shall be no bloodguilt for him, but if the sun has risen on him, there shall be bloodguilt for him. He shall surely pay. If he has nothing, then he shall be sold for his theft. If the stolen beast is found alive in his possession, whether it is an ox or a donkey or a sheep, he shall pay double.").

*

The penalty for adultery in the Torah can be found in (Leviticus 20: 10–12: "If a man commits adultery with the wife of his neighbour, both the adulterer and the adulteress shall surely be put to death. If a man lies with his father's wife,… both of them shall surely be put to death;... If a man lies with his daughter-in-law, both of them shall surely be put to death") and in (Leviticus 20: 13–16: "If a man lies with a male as with a woman... they shall surely be put to death; ... If a man takes a woman and her mother also,... he and they shall be burned with fire, ... If a man lies with an animal, he shall surely be put to death, and you shall kill the animal. If a woman approaches any animal and lies with it, you shall kill the woman and the animal").

*

Regarding apostasy in the Torah, we read in (Leviticus 20: 1-2: "The LORD spoke to Moses, saying: Say to the people of Israel, Any one of the people of Israel or of the strangers who sojourn in Israel who gives any of his children to Molech (pagan god) shall surely be put to death. The people of the land shall stone him with stones."). The penalty for sorcerers is found in (Leviticus 20: 27: "A man or a woman who is a sorcerer or a necromancer shall surely be put to death. They shall be stoned with stones; their blood shall be upon them.").

There was no penalty in the Torah for wine and alcohol drinking.

*

From the above list of penalties, we conclude that terrestrial punishments in general were more severe in Moses' Law than in the Koran's Sharia. The reason might be that in Moses' Law, Jehovah didn't disclose the reward of good people and the punishment of bad people in the afterlife, as clearly as we find it in the Koran, where we find a lengthy description of the delicacies awaiting the ones who keep their duty to Allah, and the doom of hell awaiting those who disbelieve. To remind the reader of the torment awaiting the disbelievers in hell we provide an excerpt from the Koran *(Surah 4: 56: "... Those who disbelieve in our revelations, we shall expose them to the Fire. As often as their skins are consumed, we shall exchange them for fresh skins that they may taste the torment...").* That's why we might find that killing, stoning and burning was the punishment of the Israelites during their life on Earth as no punishment awaited them in the after-life.

*

The future for humankind changed after God sent his Messiah Jesus as a mercy and a saviour from the original sin of Adam, and gave humankind hope of an eternal life with a just judgment. We read in the Evangel of (John 8: 4–11: "they said to him, 'Teacher, this woman has been caught in the act of adultery. Now in the Law, Moses' commanded us to stone such women. So what do you say?'... Jesus... stood up and said to them: 'Let him who is without sin among you be the first to throw a stone at her'. But when they heard it, they went away one by one, beginning with the older ones, and Jesus was left alone with the woman standing before him... And Jesus said: Neither do I condemn you; go, and from now on sin no more").

Regarding judgment by men we read in the Evangel of (Luke 6: 37-38: "Judge not, and you will not be judged; condemn not, and you will not be condemned; forgive, and you will be forgiven; give, and it will be given to you. Good measure, pressed down, shaken together, running over, will be put into your lap. For with the measure you use it will be measured back to you"). The Koran also mentioned the changes Jesus entered into Moses' Law as per *(Surah 3: 50: "And I come confirming that which was before me of the Torah, and to make lawful some of that which was forbidden unto you....").* That explains the measure of leniency shown in the Koran's Sharia compared with Moses' Law related to terrestrial punishments, reserving the fire punishment to God's justice in the after life.

As we mentioned in Chapter 5 B, Jesus clarified the existing difference between our duty towards God, which He summarised as loving our neighbour as we love ourselves and treating our neighbours as we wish to be treated (Matthew 7: 12), without going into the details of man-made laws, that evolve with time and vary in different locations.

He called on people not to stick to the literal wording of Moses' Law but to its spirit, and concentrate on good words and good deeds. He confirmed that perfection in faith resides in loving your neighbour as much as yourself.

From all the above exposed, we conclude that Christianity does not possess a written Law (Nomos or Sharia), apart from the Ten Commandments of God in the Torah. God's Law for humans besides the Ten Commandments of God are the Reason and the Conscience that God has placed in us, to discern good from bad and lead us to act ethically. Only the Perfect, Just and Merciful God could provide a fair judgment to humans in the afterlife, and no human has the right to punish another for a sin committed against God.

Accusing people and punishing them on the basis of their belief or disbelief in God is not right. God has sent his prophets and Jesus Christ to lead people to Him – the Absolute Truth and not to punish and/or kill them.

As regards punishment due to bad acts committed against men, it is up to the society's made laws and rules to deal with them, these man-made laws and rules are ever changing with time and location.

6. E. 5. The Zakat (Alms):

There is no rigorous definition for the amount of "Zakat" in the Koran. We read In *(Surah 9: 60: "The alms are only for the poor and the needy, and those who collect them, and those whose hearts are to be reconciled, and to free the captives and the debtors, and for the cause of Allah, and the wayfarer; a duty imposed by Allah…")*, and in *Surah 9: 103 and in (Surah 2: 215: "They ask you what they shall spend. Say that which you spend for good must go to parents and near kindred and orphans and the needy and the wayfarer. And whatsoever good you do, lo! Allah is aware of it.")*, and in *(Surah 2: 245: "Who is it that will lend to Allah a goodly loan, so that He may give it increase manifold? Allah reduces and enlarges. Unto Him you will return")* and in *(Surah 2: 274: "Those who spend their wealth by night and day, by stealth and openly, verily their reward is with their Lord, and there shall be no fear come upon them neither shall they grieve.")* and in *(Surah 64: 17: "If you lend unto Allah a goodly loan, He will double it for you and will forgive you, for Allah is Responsive, Clement.")*.

The Koran urged the faithful to give alms without stating the amount or percentage of their wealth to be given to the poor, so that each person could earn God's reward according to his intent and goodness, not depending on a specific law. Later, under pressure from Islamic state institutions who wanted to forecast the amount of Zakat (as a tax) to be acquired, certain Muslim Sharia Law doctors and scholars fixed the amount and timing of the alms to be paid under the form of "Zakat" as follows:

- Zakat has to be paid at the end of each year.
- Zakat has to be paid on certain forms of wealth.
- The percentage of Zakat shall be between 2.5% to 5.0%.

We cannot find in Moses' Law any mention about the amount of alms to be given away. We read in (Leviticus 23: 22: "And when you reap the harvest of your land, you shall not reap your field right up to its edge, nor shall you gather the gleanings after your harvest. You shall leave them for the poor and for the sojourner: I am the Lord your God.") and in (Leviticus 25: 35–37: "If your brother becomes poor and cannot maintain himself with you, you shall support him as though he were a stranger and a sojourner, and he shall live with you. Take no interest from him or profit, but fear your God, that your brother may live beside you. You shall not lend him your money at interest, nor give him your food for profit.").

6. E. 6. The "khoums" (fifth of the spoils of war) and the "Anfal":

The remittance of "Khoums" was requested in the Koran as per *(Surah 8: 41: "And know that whatever you take as spoils of war, lo! A fifth thereof is for Allah and the messenger and for the kinsman and orphans and the needy and the wayfarer…").*

The spoils of war include persons, money, land, houses, goods and other assets captured by the Muslims. The war between the Muslims and the unbelievers started when the Prophet and his companions blocked the road to a trading caravan from the tribe of Quraysh returning from Syria, headed by Abu Sufian – a rich caravan owner in Mecca, and confiscated all its goods. Later the Muslims fought many battles against the unbelievers and raided other caravans, thus helping the Prophet and the Muslim refugees after their flight to Yathrib to survive, and later to raise a well-equipped army to fight their enemies and conquer Mecca. Prophet Muhammad was later commanded by Allah to continue his wars against the other pagans tribes of the Arabian Peninsula and later, against the Jews and Christians who do not accept conversion to Islam. The spoils of war included women, children, property (land, houses, furniture), money, animals of the vanquished as per *(Surah 48: 20: "… Allah promised you much booty that you will capture, and has given you this in advance, and withheld men's hands from you, that it may be a token for the believers and that He may guide you on a right path.")* and *(Surah 8: 69: "Now enjoy the spoils you have won, as lawful and good, and keep your duty to Allah. Lo! Allah is Forgiving, Merciful.").*

According to the *Correct Hadith* of Sahih Al-Bukhari, Prophet Muhammad said: "I command you to perform four deeds: Belief in Allah, prayers upholding, alms giving (Zakat) and the remittance of "Khoums". According to Muslim scholars, the "Khoums" should be taken from the following sources:

- All spoils of war.
- Minerals and metals extracted from the ground: gold, silver, iron, oil, gas or any other minerals.
- Any money found in the ground without a known owner.

There is no mention of "Khoums" in the Old Testament.

*

The "Anfal" in the Koran is the wealth (property, money and other assets) left over by a fleeing enemy and taken without fight by the Muslims.

These spoils belong to Allah and the messenger only as per *(Surah 8: 1: "They ask you O Muhammad of the spoils of war. Say: The spoils of war belong to Allah and the messenger, so keep your duty to Allah, and solve the matter between yourselves, and obey Allah and His messenger if you are true believers").*

6. E. 7. Usury (Al-Riba):

The first mention of "Al-Riba" in the Koran was in Mecca *(Surah 30: 39: "That which you give in usury in order that it may increase other people's property has no increase with Allah; but that which you give in charity, seeking Allah's Countenance.").*

Later, when the Jews amongst whom the Muslims were living after their migration to Yathrib, requested from Muslims the payment of interest on loaned money, came the revelation in *(Surah 4: 160–161: "Because of the wrongdoing of the Jews We forbade them good things which were before made lawful unto them... And of their taking usury when they were forbidden it, and of their devouring people's wealth by false pretences. We have prepared for those of them who disbelieve a painful doom.").*

Then came the total ban on "Al-Riba" and the harsh measures against the Jews in *(Surah 2: 275–276: "Those who swallow usury cannot rise up... That is because they say: Trade is just like usury; whereas Allah permitted trading and forbade usury... As for him who returns to usury – such are owners of the Fire... Allah has blighted usury and made almsgiving fruitful. Allah loves not the impious and guilty.").*

In Moses' Law, an Israelite shall exempt a fellow Israelite from the payment of loaned money after the passage of seven years as per (Deuteronomy 15 1–4: "At the end of every seven years you shall grant a release. And this is the manner of the release: every creditor shall release what he has lent to his neighbour. He shall not exact it of his neighbour, his brother, because the Lord's release has been proclaimed. Of a foreigner you may exact it, but whatever of yours is with your brother your hand shall release. But there will be no poor among you").

Also God commanded the Israelites to lend but not to borrow money as in (Deuteronomy 15: 6: "For the Lord your God will bless you, as he promised you, and you shall lend to many nations, but you shall not borrow, and you shall rule over many nations, but they shall not rule over you.").

Not treating fellow God believing Muslims in Yathrib in accordance with Moses' Law aroused the anger of Prophet Muhammad, as he considered the migrant Arab Muslims as brothers in faith to the Jewish tribes of Yathrib, worshiping the same God, respecting the Israelite prophets, applying the Torah instructions, facing during prayers the Temple of Jerusalem. Also due to his tribe's blood ties with the Israelites, being descendants from Prophet Abraham through his first-born son Ishmael.

This might explain his harsh reaction against the Jews: the Jews in Yathrib should have at least exempted the Muslims from usury, if not exempting them from the payment of the capital after seven years of loaned money as stipulated in the Torah.

6. E. 8. Inheritance:

We read in the Koran: *(Surah 4: 11: "Allah charges you concerning the provision for your children: **to the male the equivalent of the portion of two females, and if there be women more than two, then theirs is two thirds of the inheritance, and if there be one only then the half. And to each of his parents a sixth of the inheritance, if he have a son;** and if he have no son and his parents are his heirs, then to his **mother appertains the third;** and if he have brothers, then to his mother appertains the sixth, after any legacy he may have bequeathed, or debt has been paid…").*

And *(Surah 4: 12: "And unto you belongs a half of that which your wives leave, if they have no child; but if they have a child then unto you the fourth of that which they leave, after any legacy... and **unto them belongs the fourth of that which you leave if you have no child, but if you have a child then the eighth of that which you leave,** after any legacy… And if a man or a women have a distant heir and he have a brother or a sister then to each of them twain the sixth, and if they be more than two, then they shall be sharers in the third, after any legacy… not injuring has been paid. A commandment from Allah. Allah is Knower, Indulgent.").*

*

We provide hereunder some examples, published by Mr Muhammad Hayyani in his review: *The Civilized Discussion* (محمّد حيّاني – الحوار المتحضّر) issue No. 2930 dated 28/02/2010 showing a possible interpretation of the above inheritance laws:

Example 1: A man died with two daughters, father, mother, a wife and left 1,000 Dinars.

Two daughters: *"if there be women more than two, then theirs is two thirds of the Inheritance"*: 333 + 333 = 666 Dinars.

Father and mother : *"to each of his parents a sixth of the inheritance, if he have a son"*:

166 + 166 = 333 Dinars approximately.

The wife: *"if you have a child then the eighth of that which you leave"*: 125 Dinars.

The total: 666 + 333 + 125 = **1,124 Dinars AND NOT 1,000 Dinars.**

Example 2: A man died with one daughter, father, mother, wife and left 1,000 Dinars.

The single daughter: *"if there be one only then the half"*: 500 Dinars.

Father and mother: *"to each of his parents a sixth of the inheritance, if he have a son"*:

166 + 166 = 333 Dinars approximately.

The wife: *"if you have a child then the eighth of that which you leave"*:

125 Dinars.

The total: 500 + 333 + 125 = **958 Dinars AND NOT 1,000 Dinars.**

Example 3: A man died without children, with a father, mother, a wife and left 1,000 Dinar

The mother: *"if he have no son and his parents are his heirs, then to his mother appertains the third"*: 333 Dinars.

The father: *"to the male the equivalent of the portion of two females"*: 666 Dinars.

The wife: *"unto them belongs the fourth of that which you leave if you have no child"*: 250 Dinars.

The total: 333 + 666 + 250 = **1,249 Dinars AND NOT 1,000 Dinars.**

From the results shown above, we conclude that the perfect God could not have been the initiator of these indeterminate and vague rules.

We already have discussed the status of women in D.5.2 concerning inheritance, and shown that they are not equal to men in this field. But their fate regarding inheritance in the Koran is still better than that in Moses' Law, as a daughter in Moses' Law inherits nothing in case she has a male brother as in (Numbers 27: 6–11: "… And you shall speak to the people of Israel, saying, **'If a man dies and has no son**, then you shall transfer his inheritance to his daughter. And if he has no daughter, then you shall give his inheritance to his brothers. And if he has no brothers, then you shall give his inheritance to his father's brothers. And if his father has no brothers, then you shall give his inheritance to the nearest kinsman of his clan.").

Also, The eldest son in Moses' Law inherits double his male brothers as *in* (Deuteronomy 21: 16–17: "then on the day when he assigns his possessions as an inheritance to his sons, he may not treat the son of the loved as the firstborn in preference to the son of the unloved, who is the firstborn, but **he shall acknowledge the firstborn**, the son of the unloved, **by giving him a double portion of all that he has, for he is the first fruits of his strength.** The right of the firstborn is his.")

We also read *in* (Numbers 36: 6–7: "This is what the Lord commands concerning the daughters of Zelophe: 'Let them marry whom they think best, only they shall marry within the clan of the tribe of their father. The inheritance of the people of Israel shall not be transferred from one tribe to another, …").

The Jewish Rabbis in recent times developed their inheritance rules, based on what little, Moses' Law has provided in this regard. In Christianity, women and men have equal status in inheritance laws, and in their duties and rights before men and God.

6. E. 9. Land tax "Al-Kharaj":

"Al-Kharaj" is a land tax imposed on land captured from its Christian/Jewish/pagan owners by the Arab Muslim conquerors. Al-Kharaj tax is mentioned once only in the Koran (Surah 23: 72) but in a somewhat different meaning than that given to it later. The Land tax known as Al-Kharaj was first implemented by Caliph Omar Ibn Al-Khattab, after the amount of conquered territories increased considerably, with no nomad Arab warrior having enough farming knowledge or inclination to work the land.

So in order not to partition conquered land between the Arab warriors as spoils of war with no resulting agricultural production and no benefit to the other Muslim population, he decreed that conquered land's ownership belongs to the Islamic state and could be worked by its previous owners, with its return (the Land Tax "Al-Kharaj") filling the coffers of the Islamic State administration to be shared between all Muslim citizens.

A certain number of factors influence the amount of imposed land tax. Amongst these are: Land irrigation, quality of the topsoil, frequency of its cultivation (year after year or every other year...) and its proximity to populated centres.

6. E. 10 The "Tribute" Head Tax on non-Muslims:

As we mentioned in Chapter Six, Clause D 4, the relations of Prophet Muhammad with the Jews of Yathrib worsened after their requests for interest payment "Riba" on loaned money, and their disbelief in God's revelations to him.

Accordingly, he fought them and expelled them from their homes and land in the Oasis of Yathrib and expropriated their wealth to the benefit of Allah, himself and the Muslim community. He fought later against the Jews of Khaibar and Fadak, two towns located in Hejaz, and their populations were also expelled from their homes and land, with all their wealth again benefitting Allah and the Prophet.

After the expulsion of all the Jewish population from Hejaz, the Christian population of the towns of Tabuk, Elat, Azrah and Makna, located in Southern Syria and bordering Hejaz, who until then had peaceful relations with the Muslims, were requested to convert to Islam, but refused and were obliged to pay the Tribute in order to keep their faith.

In so doing Prophet Muhammad was the first to impose the "Tribute" on the "People of the Scripture", if they don't accept conversion to Islam, basing his actions *on (Surah 9: 29–30: "Fight against such of those who have been given the Scripture as believe not in Allah nor the Last Day, and forbid not that which Allah and His messenger has forbidden , and follow not the Religion of Truth, until they pay the tribute readily, being brought low... Allah himself fought against them. How perverse are they.").*

Regarding the spoils of war, Prophet Muhammad based his action on the following revelations: *(Surah 8; 69: "Now enjoy the booty you have taken as lawful and keep your duty to Allah. Lo! Allah is forgiving, Merciful."),* and *(Surah: 48, 20: "Allah promised you much booty that you will capture, and has given you this in advance, and has withheld men's hands from you, that it may be a token for the believers, and that He may guide you on a right path.").*

The payment of "Tribute" and spoils of war were present also in Moses' Law, revealed about two thousand years before the Sharia Law, as per (Deuteronomy 20: 10-14: **"When you draw near to a city to fight against it, offer terms of peace to it. And if it responds to you peaceably and it opens to you, then all the people who are found in it shall do forced labour for you and shall serve you. But if it makes no peace with you, but makes war against you, then you shall besiege it. And when the Lord your God gives it into your hand, you shall put all its males to the sword, but the women and the little ones, the livestock, and everything else in the city, all its spoil, you shall take as plunder for yourselves. And you shall enjoy the spoil of your enemies, which the Lord your God has given you."**). Prophet Muhammad applied Moses' Law in its new versions revealed to him during his wars against his enemies and the enemies of Allah.

*

The Rashidun Caliphs who succeeded him followed the example of the "good Salaf" faithfully.

Both "AL-Kharaj" and the "Tribute" were imposed on the subdued People of the Scripture and the other pagan peoples. The tribute could be dropped after a person's conversion to Islam while the "Al-Kharaj" does not.

6. E. 11 Slavery and plunder of women:

The Koran did not prohibit trade in slaves, but indirectly encouraged it by making legal the plunder of women and children as spoils in its wars of conquest to spread Islam.

The revelations covering the Muslim rights over "whom your right hands possess" meaning captured slaves, succeeded in rapidity proportional to the military successes, spoils of war and women and children plundered by Prophet Muhammad and the Muslims against the unbelievers, as witnessed by the following revelations especially after his migration to Medina, and the multiple marriages contracted by the Prophet.

The Koran consists of two parts: the first one during the life of his first wife Khadijah and her uncle the Christian priest Waraqa Ibn Naoufal in Mecca, when his life was that of a monogamous peaceful man, the second after her death, his migration to Yathrib and his new warlike polygamous way of life besides his allies: The Aous and Khazraj Arab tribes with whom he concluded the Al-Aqaba pact, and his Jewish neighbours.

The following is a list of revelations in the Koran that cover this subject: *(Surah 16: 71: "And Allah has favoured some of you above others in provision.* **Now those who are more favoured will by no mean hand over their provision to those slaves whom they right hand possess, so they may be equal with them in respect thereof. It is then the Grace of Allah that they deny.")*

(Surah 16: 75: **"Allah gave an example: On the one hand an owned slave who has control of nothing, and on the other hand one on whom We have bestowed a fair provision from Us,** *and he spends thereof secretly and openly.* **Are they equal? Praise be to Allah!** *But most of them know not.")*

(Surah 23: 5-6: "And who guard their chastity. **Save from their wives or the slaves that their right hands possess,** *for then they are not blameworthy".)*

(Surah 70: 29–30: "And those who preserve their chastity. **Save with their wives and those whom their right hands** *possess, for then they are not blameworthy.")*

(Surah 30: 28: "He gave you as an example yourselves. **Have you from among those whom your right hand possess** **(slaves), partners in the wealth We have bestowed upon you,** *equal with you in respect thereof;* **so that you fear them as you** **fear yourselves?** *Thus we display the revelations for people who have sense.")*

(Surah 2: 178: "O you who believe! Retaliation is prescribed for you in the matter of the murdered; the freeman for the freeman, and **the slave for the slave...").**

(Surah 2: 221: "Wed not idolatresses till they believe; A **believing slave is better than an idolatress ...").**

(Surah 33: 50: **"O Prophet! We have made lawful unto** *you* **your wives** *unto whom you have paid their dowries, and* **those** **whom your right hand possess of those whom Allah has given you** **as spoils of war (slaves)** *and the daughters of your uncles on the father's side and the daughters of your aunts on the father's side, and the daughters of your uncles on the mother's side, and the daughters of your aunts on the mother's side who emigrated with you,* **and a believing woman if she gives herself unto the Prophet** **and the Prophet desires to marry her – a privilege for you only,** **not for the rest of the believers** *. We are aware of that which We enjoined upon them concerning their wives and those whom their right hands possess – that you may be free from blame.")*

(Surah 33: 52: "It is not allowed unto you (O Muhammad) to take other women henceforth, nor that you should change them for other wives even though their beauty pleased you, **save those slaves whom your right hand possessed.** *Allah is ever Watcher over all things.").*

(Surah 33: 55: "It is no sin for your wives to converse freely with their fathers, or their sons, or their brothers, or their brothers sons, or the sons of their sisters or their own women or **their slaves...").**

*(Surah 4: 3: "And if you fear that you will not deal fairly by the orphans, marry of the women , who seem good to you, two or three or four; and if you fear that you cannot do justice to so many then one only **or the captives that your right hand possess…")** .*

*(Surah 4: 25: "And who is not able to afford to marry free, believing women, let them **marry from the believing maids whom your right hand possess…").***

*(Surah 4: 92: "It is not for a believer to kill a believer unless by mistake. He who has killed a believer by mistake **must set free a believing slave**, and pay the blood money to the family of the slain…").*

*(Surah 24: 32: "And **marry such of you as are solitary and the pious of your slaves and maidservants…").***

*(Surah 24: 33: "… **Force not your slave girls to whoredom** that you may seek enjoyment of the life of the world, if they want to preserve their chastity. **And if one force them, then after their compulsion, Allah will be Forgiving, Merciful towards him .").***

*(Surah 58: 3: "Those who put away their wives and afterward would go back on that what they have said, **the penalty is the freeing of a slave** before they touch one another…").*

*(Surah 5: 89: "Allah will not ask you for that which is unintentional in your oaths, but will take you to ask for the oaths which you swear in earnest. The expiation thereof is the feeding of ten of the needy… **or the liberation of a slave…").***

In general, the above revelations requested the liberation of a slave, as expiation for certain sins as per (Surah 90: 12–13), (Surah 4: 92) and (Surah 5: 89), but did not prohibit the ownership of slaves. In fact they made the fate of slaves decided by Allah as per *(Surah 16: 71: "**Allah has favoured some of you above others in provision. Now those who are more favoured will by no mean hand over their provision to those slaves whom they right hand possess, so they may be*** *equal with them...").*We find almost the same meaning in the above mentioned (Surah 16, 75), (Surah 30, 28) and others.

Also, the revelations made it clear that the plunder of women and other captives could be achieved only by fighting the enemies of Allah and the Prophet as per *(Surah 8: 65-67: "O Prophet! Exhort the believers to fight... It is not for any prophet to have captives until he has made slaughter in the land...").* These revelations legalized the spoils of the wars of conquest by Arab and later Turkish Muslims that resulted in the ownership of thousands of slaves of various gender, religion, ethnicity and colour. Slavery existed in the Kingdom of Saudi Arabia until recent times, and possibly exists in hiding until now.

We provide hereunder the interpretation of certain Muslim scholars regarding *(Surah 4: 24: "And all married women are forbidden unto you save those captives whom your right hand possess. It is a decree of Allah for you. Lawful unto you are all beyond those mentioned ...")*:

The interpretation of Ibn Kathir:

"Save those women you plundered. It is lawful unto you to have sexual intercourse with them after the end of their menstruation." Ibn Kathir continues:

This Surah was revealed after the plunder of the Otas women (the Hanin raid, eight years after Hijrah) who were married. We were reluctant to have sexual intercourse with them as they had husbands, so we asked the Prophet (Allah bless and keep him) and this revelation was the answer. So it was legal to have intercourse with them.

The interpretation of Al-Qurtubi:

"Save the women who are plundered during war, these legally could be taken even if they have husbands." He continues:

Imam Al-Shafeei said that plunder cuts a marriage contract "… so that these women are legally your ownership after the end of menstruation…" The companions of the Prophet waited the end of a women's menstruation before having sexual intercourse. "The above revelation came unto the Prophet (Allah bless and keep him) after certain of his companions were reluctant to have intercourse with their captive women as these women were married, and Allah revealed this Surah to relieve them. The plundered woman is now owned by her new master, her marriage contract dissolved.".

The interpretation of Al-Tabari:

"Possession of your right hand: Plundered women that captivity has annulled their marriage. They are now legally owned by whoever possess them without recurring to divorce".

So the Koran didn't forbid slavery and imposed fighting on Muslims against unbelievers aiming at spreading Islam. As we know, the Rashidun Caliphs executed punctually the Koran's Sharia covering the spoils of war and plunder of women in their wars of conquest in Syria, Mesopotamia, Persia, Egypt and North Africa leading to the ownership of an ever-increasing number of slaves.

They were followed, later, by the Omayyad, Abbasid, Fatimid and Ottoman Turk Sultans. Slave women and girls, young boys and eunuchs from their dominions in Europe, Asia and Africa filled the harems of these Caliphs and later Ottoman Sultans.

The situation was not much better in Moses' Law, as it didn't forbid slavery as well. But as we mentioned in Chapter One, the slave had to be set free after seven years.

We read in the Old Testament (Exodus 21: 2–3: **"When you buy a Hebrew slave, he shall serve six years, and in the seventh he shall go out free, for nothing. If he comes in single, he shall** go out single; if he comes in married, then his wife shall go out with him."). In Hammurabi's Code of Law, which was established about 2,300 years before Prophet Muhammad's revelations, according to Law 117, the slave was freed after four years (Robert W. Rogers, *The Code of Hammurabi*, New York 1917/The Avalon Project – Documents In Law, History & Diplomacy – *The Code of Hammurabi*, Translated by L.W. King).

No reference to slaves and slavery in the New Testament, but as we mentioned in Chapter 5, Clause B, Jesus made a difference between man-made laws and Moses Law, as in (Matthew 7, 12). He made it a duty for men to behave ethically towards their brothers in humanity, dealing with them equitably, fairly and mercifully, without following Moses' Law to the letter, but its spirit.

6.F. The assembly of the Koran verses in a single book

Many Muslim scholars interpret the Koran's Arabic word "الأَمَّي" as per the translation made by Muhammad Marmaduke Picktahll, in his English translation of *The meaning of The Glorious Quran* as follows: *(Surah 7: 157: "Those who follow the messenger, the Prophet who can "neither read nor write", whom they will find described in the Torah and the Gospel which are with them…")*, meaning that Prophet Muhammad was illiterate. But the meaning of the word "الأَمَّي" is in fact: *"not acquainted with the Scriptures"*. What gives this word "الأَمَّي" it's correct meaning *is (Surah 2: 129: "Our Lord! And raise up in their midst a messenger from among them who shall recite unto them Your revelations, and shall instruct them in the Scripture and in wisdom and shall make them grow…")*. Also, as translated by Muhammad Marmaduke Picktahll in *(Surah 3: 20: "... And say unto those who have received the Scripture and unto the ones 'who read not': Have you surrendered? …")* which makes it clear that the Arabic word "الأَمَّي" means *"those who haven't received the Scripture"* and not the ones *"who read not"*. But especially *(Surah 87: 6: "We shall make you read O Muhammad so that you will not forget.")*,

*

The Arab pagans didn't accuse him of illiteracy but of good writing skills as in *(Surah 25: 5: "And they say: Fables and myths of the men of old which he has had written down so that they are dictated to him morn and evening")*.

And how could Prophet Muhammad have been an illiterate, he who travelled extensively with the caravans to Roman Southern Syria, was such a successful and trustful tradesman that the rich Khadija Bint Khouelid – the woman owner of caravans was attracted to marry him, becoming thereafter the manager of her caravans. And how could a successful tradesman be illiterate when he has to calculate his expenses and profits and write commercial agreements!

Prophet Muhammad was keen to write the "revelations" during his stay in Mecca, and we know from his companions that after his migration to Yathrib, he entrusted the writing of his "revelations" to Zaid Bin Thabet Al-Ansari, who had better writing skills than the Prophet, and the Prophet often asked him to read them to him. Also, he entrusted to him the task of learning the Hebrew language (the Bible was written in Hebrew) as it was the language of the Jewish Rabbis of Yathrib. Zaid himself is referred to have said: "the Prophet requested me to learn the Jewish Rabbis language, as he said: I do not trust them with my book". And according to certain sources (Al-Turmuzi, Abou Daoud), Prophet Muhammad requested him to learn the Syriac/Aramean language, as it was the language of the Evangels in Christian Syria (Jesus spoke Aramean). Zaid would read to him the Bible, his letters to the Jewish Rabbis and their answers to him (Al-Tabari's History).

Zaid Bin Thabet read twice the "revelations" that he wrote to Prophet Muhammad during the last year before Prophet Muhammad's death, and that reading was later called "Zaid's reading" as he was the one who wrote and read it.

Many of Prophet Muhammad's companions as Ali Ibn Abi Taleb, Abdallah Massoud, Ubai bin Ka'b and others have memorized as many of the Koran's verses as they could. During the life of Prophet Muhammad, the Koran verses were written on skins, pieces of tissue, bones and stones. After the end of the Yamama wars with the death of many of Muhammad's companions who memorized the Koran, Omar Ibn Al-Khatab asked Caliph Abou Bakr to assemble the Koran verses before the death of the remaining companions. The Caliph called Zaid Ibn Thabet and requested him to assemble what he could of the Koran verses. Zaid was reported saying his famous words on this subject: "By Allah it would have been easier for me to move a mountain, than to assemble the Koran verses".

Zaid also said: "I was gathering the verses from pieces of tissue, skins, bones and men's memories". He assembled certain revelations on many pieces of material (Al-Seera of Ibn Hisham, Al-Tabari's History).

During the Caliphate of Othman Ibn Affan, Othman and the remaining companions of the Prophet decided to assemble the many existing pieces in a single volume, as some parts had duplicated surahs with different number of verses, and the danger of loss and alterations was increasing. So Othman inquired about the best available writer and the companions answered: "Zaid Ibn Thabet – the man charged by the Prophet to write his revelations", and who is the best in Arabic oratory skills inquired Othman, they answered: "Sa'eed Ibn Al-Ass", and Othman commanded: "let Sa'eed dictate and Zaid write". Zaid with his companions went to the house of Hafsa the daughter of Caliph Omar Ibn Al-Khattab and collected whatever written verses of the Koran she had, as well as the other available pieces he has written, and assembled them into a single book in three copies. A copy was sent to Damascus, a second one to Kufa in Iraq and the third copy was kept in Medina.

On this subject, we should report that some persons spread rumours that these so called "revelations" to Prophet Muhammad were not in fact of a divine source but were copied from the Bible, and these rumours were countered in certain verses of the Koran as *in (Verse 4–5 of Surah 25: "Those who disbelieve say: This is naught but a lie that has been invented, **and other folk have helped him with it**, so that they have produced a slander and a lie. And they say: **Fables and myths of the men of old which he has written down, that they are dictated to him morn and evening"), also in (Verse 103 of Surah 16: "And we know well that they say: Only a man taught him. The speech of him at whom they falsely hint is foreigner, and this is clear Arabic speech.").*

6. G. Are the Koran verses revealed word by word by Allah?

There is no way to deny that Prophet Muhammad had knowledge of the Bible due to his contacts with the Christian clergy and Jewish Rabbis. As we mentioned in Chapter 6 C, the uncle of Khadija, his first wife, Waraka Ibn Naoufal was a Christian priest (monk) in Mecca, and certain early Muslim sources report that Waraka did translate the Bible into Arabic.

Prophet Muhammad's acquaintance with the Bible occurred also during his travels to the town of Bosra in Southern Syria and his meetings with the Christian Arian monk Bahira, and his subsequent meetings and correspondence with Jewish Rabbis in Yathrib as reported by Zaid Ibn Thabet Al-Ansari in Chapter 6 F, and confirmed by Allah in *(Verse 103 of Surah 16: "And we know well that they say: Only a man taught him. The speech of him at whom they falsely hint is foreigner, and this is clear Arabic speech.")* .

An additional proof about Prophet Muhammad's knowledge of the Torah and the Evangels is found in the Koran as Allah specifically requested it from him as in *(Surah 10: 94: "So if you are in doubt, [O Muhammad], about that which We have revealed to you, then ask those who have been reading the Scripture before you. The truth has certainly come to you from your Lord, so never be among the doubters")*.

This verse categorically indicates that Prophet Muhammad had knowledge of the Bible, and confirms that the Bible (Old and New Testament) were not altered at the time of Muhammad, as Allah wouldn't have commanded him to ask those who have been reading the Scripture, to ascertain the correctness of what was revealed to him, contradicting some Muslim scholars who proclaim nowadays, that the cause of Allah's command to fight Christians and Jews was their alteration of the Scripture. It indicates that Prophet Muhammad with his logical analytical mind reviewed the different *interpretations* of the evangels by Christian clergymen of different sects that he met, and also later during his contacts with the Jewish Rabbis in Yathrib, came to appreciate the Torah that contained the Law of Moses which was close to the way of life of his tribal people, and reached certain conclusions that he tried to express in a book "revealed" to him in Arabic language to serve as a guide to his people, where he tried to correct the *misinterpretations* of the others, and where he lead a solid religious and legislative basis for the establishment of a Muslim Arab state, where religious beliefs and a terrestrial legislation fused into a single entity.

*

Going through the Koran verses, we notice that Zaid Ibn Thabet assembled without any chronological order, Prophet Muhammad's revelations that occurred during a period exceeding twenty–two years, a fact that makes it difficult for the reader to understand the relationship between the historical events and the cause for the appearance of each of these revelations. He placed the all-important, from a legislative point of view, and lately revealed lengthy Medina Muslim State building Surahs, at the start of the Koran (Surah 1, 2, 3, 4, 5), while he left certain Meccan Surahs in the middle and assembled most of the short Meccan Surahs at the end of the Koran, although they were the first ones to be revealed to Muhammad.

*

Zaid assembled also with the "revealed" verses others that can only be supplications to Allah by Prophet Muhammad as in *(Surah 2: 286: "... Our Lord! Condemn us not if we forget, or miss the mark! Our Lord! Lay not on us such a burden as You did lay on those before us! Our Lord! Impose not on us that which we have not the strength to bear! Pardon us, absolve us and have mercy on us, You, our Protector, and give us victory over the disbelieving folk."),* and in *(Surah 3: 193–194: "… Our Lord! Therefor forgive us our sins, and remit from us our evil deeds, and make us die the death of the righteous. Our Lord! And give us that which You have promised to us by Your messengers. Confound us not upon the Day of Resurrection…")* and other verses.

*

He also assembled some contradictory verses as in *(Surah 23: 1 4: "… So blessed be Allah, the Best of Creators!")* that shows Allah as being the best of many creators, which goes against a main Muslim belief that Allah is the only Creator. But we cannot place much blame on Zaid as it was a bit difficult for him to differentiate between what Prophet Muhammad reported as being a revelation and what the prophet did say on his own, especially that he undertook the assembly of all these so called "revelations" (revealed to Prophet Muhammad during a period of about twenty-two years), more than twenty years after the death of the Prophet, with all what he faced collecting these revelations from different pieces of material and sources as explained in Chapter 6.F.

*

There are in the Koran verses that Allah (God) couldn't have been the initiator, as it goes counter the absolute and infinite Power, Perfection, Goodness, Mercifulness, Fairness and Justice of God, as *(Verse 54 of Surah 3: "And the disbelievers schemed, and Allah schemed against them: and **Allah is the best of Schemers**."),* also *(Verse 50–51 of Surah 27: "**So they plotted a plot: and We plotted a plot**, while they perceived not. Then see the nature of the consequence of their plotting, for Lo! We destroyed them and their people, every one."),* also *(Verse 99 of*

*Surah 7: "Are they then secure from **Allah's scheme**? None deems himself secure from **Allah's scheme** save folk that perish.")*. The All-Powerful God does not need to be cunning, plotting and scheming to carry out his wishes. It is sufficient for Him to say "be" for His wish to be executed. Many Muslims use the good attributes of God in giving names to their children. Even the simplest minded person in Arab Muslim countries would refuse to name his son: **"The slave of the Schemer** عبد الماكر**"**, as it is not one of the many good attributes of Allah.

Also we find certain other verses in the Koran that contradict the goodness and mercifulness of Allah as in: (Verse 22–23 of Surah 8: **"*Lo! The worst of beasts in Allah's sight are the deaf, the dumb, who have no sense. Had Allah known of any good in them He would have made them hear, but had He made them hear they would have turned away, averse*"**. And Verse 17 of Surah 18: **"*… He whom Allah guides, he indeed is led right, and he whom He sends astray, for him you will not find a guiding friend.*"**.

And Verse 97 of Surah 17: **"*And he whom Allah guides, he is led right; while, as for him whom He sends astray, for them you will find no protecting friends beside Him, and We shall assemble them on the day of Resurrection on their faces, … their habitation will be hell; whenever it abates, We increase the flame for them*"**.

And Verse 3–4 of Surah 76: "Lo! *We have guided him (man), whether he be grateful or disbelieving. Lo! We have prepared for disbelievers manacles and carcans and a raging fire*".

And Verse 6–7 of Surah 2: "As for the disbelievers, whether you warn them or you warn them not it is all one for them; they believe not. *Allah has sealed their hearing and their hearts, and on their eyes there is a covering. Theirs will be an awful doom.*".

And Verse 155 of Surah 7: "*… It is but your Temptation You send astray whom You wilt and guides whom You wilt…*".

And Verse 16 of Surah 17: *"And when We want to destroy a town We send commandment to its folk who live at ease, to commit abomination therein, and so the word is justified for it, and We annihilate it completely"*.

The above verses depict Allah as controlling the fate of man before his creation. He is the one who leads man to good deeds and He is the one who leads him to his loss. He is the one who creates the blind and deaf, viewed by Allah as being the worst of beasts, whose destination is hell, without Allah giving a free will to man to escape from his fate. The conclusion therefore is that Allah is not just and merciful with his creation, as when He creates a person He has already condemned him to either paradise or hell, which contradicts what our logic would assume the Perfect, Just and Merciful God to be, and the above verses also contradict some other verses of the Koran that give a different description of Allah.

We therefore have the right to ask ourselves: Are these Koran verses revealed by Allah or are they what Prophet Muhammad himself said in different circumstances? understood by mistake by his companions as been revealed? And how easily could they have differentiated what has been revealed to him from what has been said by him? We could extend the same question to all other verses commanding Muslims to terrorize and fight the disbelievers and the People of the Scripture who refused to convert to Islam. As the all Just, Loving and Merciful Allah couldn't have sent a prophet and commanded him to kill any of His creatures, He who gave Prophet Moses His Ten Commandments that included: "Do not kill". The all-Mighty God if He wanted wouldn't have created an unbeliever, but He gave people their freedom of belief by creating them with a conscience and reason and sent the Prophets and His Messiah to guide them and not to kill them.

We can also refer to (Verse 116 of Surah 5: *"When Allah said: O Jesus, son of Mary! Did you say unto mankind: Take me and my mother for two gods besides Allah? He said: Be glorified! It was not mine to utter that to which I had no right. If I used to say it, then You knew it. You know what is in my mind, and I know not what is in Your Mind...").* We should mention here that no Christian believes that the Virgin Mary is another god, and no Christian Church ever did express this idea as it does not have a basis in the Evangels and other canonical Christian literature.

Also what we have exposed in clause 6. E. 8. regarding the presence of calculation inaccuracies in Sharia's Inheritance Laws, contradicting the perfection of God.

Another contradiction covers the need for Allah to abrogate certain verses to replace them with better ones as in (Verse 106 in Surah 2: **"Nothing of Our revelation do we abrogate or cause be forgotten, but We bring in place one better or the like thereof. Know you not that Allah is able to do all things?"**), as our understanding of the absolutely Perfect God is that whatever he reveals should be absolutely perfect, and no need to replace it with a better one. Also in *(Verse 39 of Surah 13:* **"Allah cancels what He will (of His revelations), and confirms (what He will), and with Him is the source of the Book."***).* Here Allah cancelled some of his revelations and confirmed others, according to the political situation and changing circumstances and undertaken actions by his prophet Muhammad. Also in *(Verse 7 of Surah 3:* **"He it is who has revealed unto you (Muhammad) the Scripture some of which are clear revelations – They are the mother of the book – and others which are allegorical. But those in whose hearts is doubt pursue that which is allegorical seeking to cause dissension and strife by seeking to explain it. None knows its explanation save Allah.** *And those who are of sound knowledge say: We believe therein; the whole is from our Lord...").*The question here is: Does the All-Merciful God wants to reveal to his creatures some clear and other "allegorical" somewhat similar or contradictory verses which could lead to strife and dissension between his believers?

*

Until today, no Muslim authority, doctor in Sharia Law, imam or scholar has been able to separate the "mother of the book" revelations from the "allegorical" revelations. Instead, we hear and read every day contradicting "fatwas" from different sheikhs and imams, basing their view on this verse or that verse of the Koran, varying between extremists, moderates and liberals. The extremists (Wahabi Muslims, Al-Qaeda, Al-Nusra, Somali Al-Shabab, Nigeria's Boko Haram etc...) basing their views on certain Koran verses, are calling for the establishment of an Islamic state based on Sharia Law, using brute force to reach their goals, killing the unbelievers and other Muslims wherever they are if they do not convert to their correct version of Islam, with the resulting plunder of wealth, women and children, as per the good example of the "the good salaf". The "moderates" (the Muslim Brotherhood, Ahrar Al-Sham, Jaish Al-Islam, etc...) strive to reach political power by any means in order to accomplish their program. Their program includes the application of certain verses of the Sharia Law. They call outwardly for the spread of Islam by democratic means, while their real and final goal once they reach political power is to establish an Islamic state, and to spread Islam through military, economic and administrative punitive sanctions (including terror) on non-Muslims, as was the norm in the early Islamic Caliphate . The "liberals" (secular minded Muslims) call to keep religion separate from politics, concentrating on good deeds and Allah's worship. Each of these factions is basing its views on this or that verse of the Koran, the Al-Hadith and Prophet Muhammad's way of life (Sunnah).

6. H. Sects in Islam

The most serious schism in Islam appeared in AD 656 after the assassination of Caliph Othman Ibn Affan. The aristocratic Omayyad house accused Ali Ibn Abi Taleb (the cousin of Prophet Muhammad) and his supporters, of Caliph Othman's assassination, on the ground that Ali claimed the Caliphate for himself in AD 644 after the assassination of Caliph Omar Ibn Al-Khattab, before the election of Othman to the Caliphate.

The supporters of Ali thought then that Ali was the best placed for the Caliphate, as he was the Muslims Imam in prayer, a close companion to the Prophet, a Koran memoriser as well as the Prophet's cousin, the husband of the Prophet's only living daughter Fatima, and the father of the Prophet's only grandchildren Al-Hasan and Al-Husein.

Even before Caliph Othman's killing, Ali Ibn Abi Taleb, Talha Ibn Oubeid Allah and Al-Zubeir Ibn Al-Aouam had condemned certain of Caliph Othman's actions, namely the appointment of his Omayyad relatives as governors of Egypt and Iraq, and as head of the state treasury. The opposition led by Ali Ibn Abi Taleb organized a strong rally in the town of Kufa in Iraq, and from Kufa the rebellion spread to Egypt and from there the rebels marched to Medina and surrounded the Caliph in his house in AD 656. The son of the first Muslim Caliph Abou Bakr Al-Saddiq killed Caliph Othman in his house. The rebel leaders and their followers proclaimed Ali Ibn Abi Taleb as the new Muslim Caliph.

A fight broke out after the appointment of Ali as Caliph. Its aim was the seizure of the political and economic power in the newly expanding Arab Muslim State, whose conquered territories and war spoils has increased considerably within a short period of time, between three Qurashi houses: The Omayyad aristocratic house and the Hashemite house with its two branches: Ali Ibn Abi Taleb – the cousin of the Prophet and Abdallah Ibn Al-Abbas – the other cousin of the Prophet.

At the beginning, the winner was the Omayyad house, as Caliph Othman, who was an Omayyad, succeeded in appointing his relatives to governorships of Egypt and Iraq and the state treasury as we have reported earlier. His other Omayyad relative Mu'awia Ibn Abi Sufiyan was already governor of Syria.

After the ascension of Ali to the Caliphate, his previous allies Talha and Al-Zoubeir rose against him, besides Aisha the young widow of Prophet Muhammad. Ali defeated them in Al-Jamal battle close to Basra in Iraq in AD 656 after which, Ali established his capital in Kufa – Iraq. Mu'awia Ibn Abi Sufiyan – the Omayyad governor of Syria who didn't recognize Ali as new Caliph, demanded that Ali to punish the killers of his relative Caliph Othman. As Caliph Ali couldn't satisfy the demand of Mu'awia, as the killer was his ally, war broke out between the two sides. The war besides the declared goal of punishing the killers was in fact a fight for the control of the power centre of the new Arab Muslim State: Kufa in Iraq – the old residence of the kings of the Persian Sassanid Empire or Damascus in Syria, the capital of the East Roman Byzantine province.

During the battle of Saffin which took place between the two parties, the commander of Mu'awia's army Amr Ibn Al-Ass, foreseeing that the result of the battle was not in his favour, demanded arbitration to take place. The declared goal of the arbitration was to spare the blood of the Muslims and a later date for the arbitration was fixed in order to be attended by a number of the Prophet's companions.

During Caliph Ali's return to Kufa, twelve thousand men of his army (called later Khawarej) rebelled against him refusing the arbitration, declaring that: "The book of Allah has already settled the dispute condemning these usurpers", by "usurpers" they meant governor Mu'awia and his followers, and that no arbitration should have been accepted by Caliph Ali.

The result of the arbitration that took place later, with the presence of four hundred witnesses from each side, was the destitution of both Caliph Ali and governor Mu'awia (Al-Yakoubi Vol. 2 page 220–222), (Al-Tabari Vol. 1 page 334–36). Following that destitution, a Khawarej rebel killed Caliph Ali in Kufa on 24th January AD 661.

After his death, Caliph Ali Ibn Abi Taleb became a most revered martyr for his Shia supporters (the word shia means sect in Arabic and it was later used to cover Caliph Ali's followers), and Shia Muslims became the deadliest enemies of Mu'awia and the Omayyad Caliphs who succeeded him. The place of his assassination in Najaf became one of two most important pilgrimage centres for Shia Muslims.

After the destitution of Caliph Ali, Mu'awia succeeded through strong backing from his supporters to be elected as Caliph in Jerusalem in AD 660, establishing his capital in Damascus. According to Sunni historians, he was able to obtain from the sons of Caliph Ali: Al-Hasan and Al-Hussein a renunciation from any claim concerning their right to the caliphate. He died in AD 680.

Before his death, he was able to secure the caliphate's succession to his son Yazid, and that was an important event in Arab Muslim history, as it was the Omayyad Caliph Mu'awia who introduced the hereditary monarchical principle in Muslim political life, in contradiction to the first four Caliphs who were elected by the people.

6. H. 1 Shia Muslim Sects

Shia Muslims consider Caliph Mu'awia and his Omayyad successors as usurpers from the right to the caliphate of Al-Hasan and Al-Hussein, the sons of Caliph Ali Ibn Abi Taleb. They claim that Mu'awia forced Al-Hasan to renounce his right to the Caliphate, as Al-Hasan didn't have the military might to stand-up to Mu'awia, and feared treason from some of his army generals. They also claim that Al-Hasan accepted Mu'awia's accession to the Caliphate on the following conditions: That Mu'awia should not persecute Caliph Ali's supporters, should not curse Caliph Ali during Friday prayers, and that he and his brother Al-Hussein should succeed Mu'awia as caliphs. According to Shia Muslims, Mu'awia reneged on this agreement, as he continued to curse Caliph Ali during Friday prayers, sent a killer to poison Al-Hasan and named his son Yazid to succeed him.

After the accession of Yazid, the son of Mu'awia to the Caliphate, the Shia supporters of Caliph Ali rebelled in Iraq and demanded from Al-Hussein, the younger brother of Al-Hasan, to claim the Caliphate, as his elder brother Al-Hasan had died in the meantime. Al-Hussein, at the insistence of his supporters in Iraq, moved with his family and companions to Kufa in Iraq, but before reaching Kufa was met at a location called Karbala by the Omayyad army, who killed him and his companions and sent their heads to Caliph Yazid in Damascus, alongside the women and children of Al-Hussain's house (Ibn Asaker Vol.4 page 332–335), (Ibn Al-Athir Vol. 4 page 67–75). The day of Al-Hussein's killing (the 10th of Muharram 61 of Al-Hijra) became a day of mourning for Shia Muslims (Yaoum Ashura). Each year, millions of Shia pilgrims flock to Karbala to mark their deep sorrow for having left Imam Al-Hussein (the grandson of the Prophet) an easy prey to his Omayyad enemies. Yom Ashura confirmed Shia Muslims belief in the legal right of the descendants of Prophet Muhammad to the Caliphate, and they became the sworn opponents of the Omayyad Caliphs.

Many Persian converts to Islam also joined the Shia rebels, as Imam Al-Hussain's only wife – Shahr Banu was the daughter of Yazdajard Anu Shirvan – the last Sassanid king of Persia (she was made captive by the Arab Muslim army after the rout of the Persian army at Qadissia, and was later freed by Imam Ali Ibn Abi-Taleb and given as wife to his younger son Al-Hussain), therefore the descendants of Al-Hussain had Persian roots. Another cause of their discontent was that the Omayyad caliphs refused to relieve them from tribute payment after their conversion to Islam.

Iraqi Arab and Persian Shia Muslims became the biggest opponents to the Omayyad Caliphs rule as they considered them usurpers and hypocrites. Their frequent rebellions continued against the Omayyad Caliphate. Besides their loathing of the Omayyads, another cause of Iraqi Shia Muslims discontent was the Omayyad caliph's transfer of the capital and seat of government to Damascus in Syria instead of Kufa in Iraq.

After the tragic death of Al-Hussein, the following Imams – descendants of Al-Hussein, succeeded him: Ali Zein Al-Abidin and his two sons: Muhammad Al-Baqer and Zaid. Zaid again rose against the Omayyad rule, repeating the experience of his grandfather Al-Hussein (he believed that the right of Ali Ibn Abi-Taleb to the caliphate was bigger than the first Caliph Abi- Bakr Al-Siddiq but didn't consider him an usurper), during the caliphate of Hisham Ibn Abdel Malek, and ended in his killing. His followers formed a sect based on his beliefs known in history as the Zaidi Sect (this sect followers live at present mostly in Yemen). Muhammad Al-Baqer, the elder brother of Zaid died eight years before Zaid's killing (in AD 736), and left a son: Jaafar Al-Sadeq.

Abdallah Abu Al-Abbas, the grandson of the Prophet's uncle, taking advantage of the state of weakness of the successors of the Omayyad Caliph Hisham, and the military weakness of the Omayyad army after the dispatch of a big contingent of the Syrian Army to Al-Andalus (Spain) and the disaffection of Shia Muslims in Iraq, declared that the Hashemite house of Prophet Muhammad has more right to the caliphate (the Prophet's succession) than the Omayyad aristocratic house and called for the downfall of the Omayyad dynasty. He moved to Kufa, the centre of the Shia rebellion against the Omayyad Caliphate to prepare the uprising. Meanwhile, Abu Muslim Al-Khorasani had started his rebellion against the Omayyad governor of Khorasan – Persia, and was joined by crowds of disaffected Persian Shia. The Omayyad governor of Khorasan found himself unable to crush the rebellion, and the towns of Meroe, Nahawand and Kufa fell to the hands of the rebels who proclaimed Abu Al-Abbas Caliph in Kufa on 30th October AD 749. Abu Al-Abbas became the founder of the Abbasid Dynasty.

The Shia Muslims who assisted Abu Al-Abbas to overthrow the Omayyad rule were disappointed to find out that Caliph Abu Al-Abbas kept the caliphate on hereditary lines as did the Omayyad caliphs previously, while their goal was for the caliphate to devolve to one of the descendants of Imam Ali. Anew, they rose against the Abbasid Caliphate, forming a party known as the "Talibeyeen" (reference to Ali Ibn Abi-Taleb). The Abbasid caliphs didn't treat Shia Muslims any better than the previous Omayyad caliphs, and continued using the hereditary monarchical principle, established by the Omayyad caliphs, to perpetuate their hold on political power. They continued the persecution of Shia Muslims by killing the sons of Imam Al-Hasan: Muhammad surnamed "Pure Spirit" and crucified him in AD 762, and decapitated his brother Ibrahim in AD 763, after which Caliph Haroun Al-Rashid exterminated the Baramika clan – the Persian allies of Shia Muslims in AD 803.

Imam Jaafar Al-Sadeq died in AD 770 and left a son named Imam Moussa Al-Qazem, the later died leaving a number of children, the eldest was Ali Ibn Moussa Al-Rida.

The famous Abbasid Caliph, Al-Ma'moun, thought to satisfy the demand of the "Talibeyeen", who required the caliphate to devolve to the Hashemite family branch of Ali Ibn Abi Taleb, and not to the branch of Abu Al-Abbas, and named Ali Ibn Moussa Al-Rida as Crown Prince, provoking strong reactions from Abbasid ranks. But Ali Al-Rida died suddenly in 825 AD raising rumours by the "Talibeyeen" that his killing was ordered by Caliph Al-Ma'moun, causing the "Talibeyeen" to continue their unabated rebellion against the Abbasids, as it was previously against the Omayyads.

The son of Ali Al-Rida named Muhammad Al-Jawad died in AD 842 leaving a son named Ali Ibn Mohammad Al-Hadi, who died in AD 876. He had a son named Al-Hasan Ibn Ali, nicknamed Al-Askari, who died leaving only a five years old son named Muhammad. Muhammad died suddenly and Shia Muslims claim that he "disappeared from view".

The Shia opposition to the Abbasid caliphs rule found a sympathetic echo in Persia, where the population, after years of Arab Muslim dominance, felt humiliated remembering the glorious days of the ancient Persian Empires, seeing their culture and people subdued and ruled by backward Arab nomads. Another cause of Persian Shia Muslims opposition to Arab rule was that the descendants of Imam Al-Hussain were also the descendants of Persian King Yazdajard (through his daughter Shahr Banu – the only wife of Al-Hussain). They found in the rebellions of the "Talibeyeen" Shia an appropriate answer to their ambitions, and they joined them in order to bring down the Abbasid Caliphate, using in their interpretation of Islam, a Persian pragmatic way of thinking, relying on the Koran only as sole source of revelation, rejecting the Al-Hadith (Prophet Muhammad's talk) as having been corrupted by many generations of oral transmission and mixed up with the customs and traditions of backward nomad Arabs.

The Shia schools of thought, formed gradually in time, the most important of these in existence today are listed as follows:

a. **The Zaidi Sect**

Zaid Ibn Ali Zein-Al-Abideen rose against the Omayyad rule, assembling around him many Shia Muslims. He was killed during the caliphate of Hisham Ibn Abdel Malek, in tragic circumstances, not too different from those of his grandfather Al-Hussein. After his death, part of Shia Muslims split refusing to see the Imamate devolving to his brother Muhammad Al-Baqer, who was considered by most Shia as being their Imam.

This sect was known as the Zaidi Sect, in reference to Zaid. This sect differs from the other Shia sects as it believes that the imamate do not belong specifically to the eldest son of a senior Imam, but to any male descendent from Imam Ali Ibn Abi Taleb who would fight for it. Among their Imams is Yahya Ibn Zaid Ibn Ali, Muhammad "Pure Spirit" son of Al-Hasan and others. Abu Faraj Al-Isfahani, the author of *Fights of the Talebeyeen* and *Al-Aghani Book* used poetry and subtle style trying to gain the hearts and minds of Muslims to the painful fate of Prophet Muhammad's descendants.

The majority of Sunni Muslims believe the Zaidi Sect to be closer to them ideologically than the other Shia sects, as the Zaidi Sect do not consider the caliphs Abu Bakr, Omar and Othman as usurpers, but prefer Ali to have been named Caliph in their stead, contrary to the beliefs of other Shia Muslims.

b. **The Twelve Imami Shia Sect**

They believe in the following twelve infallible Imams: 1. Ali Ibn Abi Taleb, 2. Al-Hasan Ibn Ali, 3. Al-Hussein Ibn Ali, 4. Ali Zein Al-Abideen, 5. Muhammad Al-Baqer Ibn Zein Al-Abideen, 6. Jaafar Al-Sadeq Ibn Muhammad Al-Baqer, 7. Mousa Al-Kazem, 8. Ali Al-Rida, 9. Muhammad Al-Jawad, 10. Ali Al-Hadi,

11. Al-Hasan Ibn Ali Al-Askari, 12. Muhammad Ibn Hasan Al-Askari.

They believe that Muhammad Ibn Hasan Al-Askari (the 12th Imam) is "Al-Mahdi" who disappeared from view, but will return at the end of days to fill the world with Justice.

Their beliefs:

- The heredity principle in the transmission of the Imamate from Imam Ali Ibn Abi Taleb to his sons and their descendants, starting from the eldest son.
- The infallibility of these Imams, and that their interpretation of the Koran is as correct as the Koran itself and the Prophet's Al-Hadith.
- They believe that the Koran was altered while assembling it, and that there were verses that were cancelled and others added, as reported by Al-Tubrusi in his book: (فصل الخطاب في تحريف كتاب رب الأرباب) (*The Alterations of God's Book*) and other Shia literature.
- Their loathing of the first three Muslim caliphs: Abu Bakr, Omar and Othman as well as Mu'awia calling them usurpers, as well as Aisha and Hafsa (the wives of Prophet Muhammad) and some other companions of the Prophet.
- Their belief in the reappearance of the 12th Imam at the End of Days.

The Twelve Imami Shia sect is the most numerous Shia sect in the world today, as it represents about 85% of the Shia population. More than two thirds of the Shia world population lives in Iran, Iraq and Azerbaijan. Historians claim that the high presence of Shia Muslims in these three countries is due to the rule of the Safawid Dynasty in Iran (AD 1501–1736), after the accession of Ismail Al-Safawi to power, and his imposition of the Twelve Imami Shia Sect as sole official religion in the country.

Imam Jaafar Al-Sadeq laid the basis of the Shia jurisprudence and spread it between his followers. Thousands of disciples studied at his school and followed his teaching. Shia Muslims consider him one of the most brilliant scholars of the Muslim Nation. That's the reason why many call this sect also: "The Jaafari Sect"

c. **The Alawite Sect**
This sect is a branch of the Twelve Imami or Jaafari Sect and what makes it different from the Twelve Imami Sect is its belief in the esoteric (Batini: hidden meaning) interpretation of the Koran. Some Sunni Muslims call this sect the "Nusairi Sect". The Alawites believe that Muhammad Ibn Nusair Al-Numairi was one of the representatives of Imam Al-Mahdi during his disappearance (Sheikh Muhammad Al-Sanad, the representation during the disappearance, Vol. 1 page 11) and according to certain researchers, they base their doctrine on Shia Muslim sources, but also on the "Majmou'" book consisting of 16 surats and the "Bakoura" and "Nuzom Al-Deeniya" books. Due to the excessive secrecy of this sect, many accusations were historically directed to its followers, some Shia Muslims even calling them extremists in their sanctification of Imam Ali (Martin Creamer, *Syrian Alawites and the Shia*), while some Sunni Muslims call them the "Batini Sect unbelievers'. They live in the Syrian coastal mountains and in Southern Turkey.

After the death of Imam Hasan Al-Askari, his five years old son Imam Muhammad Ibn Hasan Al-Askari (Al-Mahdi) disappeared, but despite his disappearance, he was answering questions sent to him via four middle men called by Shia Muslims "The Imam's ambassadors" covering religious matters. One group of Shia Muslims believed that Muhammad Ibn Nusair Al-Numairi is the "Access Door" to Imams Al-Hasan Al-Askari and his son Muhammad Al-Mahdi (The Alawiyeen Site, the proof of Abou Shouaib Muhammad Ibn Nusair's access, Sheikh Hussein Muhammad Mazloum). Other Muslims called them "the Nusairi Sect" while they call themselves: Alawites.

The Alawites differ from the Twelve Imami Shia Sect in their interpretations of the Koran, and their sanctification of Imam Ali Ibn Abi Taleb, the cousin of Prophet Muhammad. The Alawite Sheiks believe that they know the correct hidden meaning of the Koran verses and they base their Koran interpretation on Reason. According to them, the root of the word "knowledge" is the verb "to know" which means understand through Reason, and that knowledge precedes faith, as it is impossible to believe in something without knowing it. They base their beliefs on what Ali Ibn Abi Taleb said in certain of his speeches: "knowledge comes before belief". The Alawites belief is to find God through reason, to follow His instructions and to submit to Him. They follow the reasoning methods of Greek philosophers, mainly Plato, in their knowledge of God, his prophets and followers.

The Alawite Sect might be classified under the "Submission to the Twelve Imams" Shia group of sects. These Imams are the descendants of Prophet Muhammad through his cousin Ali Ibn Abi Taleb and his daughter Fatima.

They base their Koran interpretation on *(verse 124 of Surah 2: "… He said: Lo! I have appointed you an Imam for mankind. Abraham said:….")* and *(verse 71* of Surah 17: *"... On the day when We shall summon all men with their Imams..."*) and (*verse 5 of Surah 28: "And We desired to show favour unto those who were oppressed in the earth and to make them Imams and to make them the inheritors"*).

Also, on the speech of Prophet Muhammad giving to Ali the authority to rule after him: "... He is my brother, my minister and my successor and inheritor after me, so listen to him and obey him..." and Prophet Muhammad's speech at Gadir Khum: "to whom I am a leader, Ali is his leader, may God succour his securer and punish his enemy and give victory to whoever helps him...". Alawites believe also in the incarnation of spirits.

The Alawite Sect is surrounded with mystery, as there is not any known organization responsible to spread the teachings of this sect. Due to the scarcity of the publications about it, the sect with its beliefs remains surrounded in shrouds of secrecy, as the sect keeps its publications within a very limited sphere of senior persons, contrary to the practice of other sects. A closed circle of people keep the teachings of this sect outside the reach of others.

d. **The Ismaelites Sect**

After the death of Imam Jaafar Al-Sadeq, most Shia Muslims declared his son Mousa Al-Kazem the new Imam, but some Shia Muslims believed that the Imamate should devolve to his elder brother Ismael Ibn Jaafar Al-Sadeq, even if he died while his father was still alive, and refused the imamate of Mousa Al-Kazem. A second schism within the Shia sect appeared, known as the Ismaelite Sect.

The Ismaelite were renowned for their activity, as they were the only Shia Muslims who succeeded to establish a powerful state: the Fatimid Caliphate, a strong opponent to the Abbasid Caliphate, a long time after the tragic end of the Caliphate of Ali Ibn Abi Taleb.

The Ismaelites believed that Imam Muhammad Al-Habib was the son of Imam Ismael Ibn Jaafar Al-Sadeq's grandson. Muhammad Al-Habib lived in Salamyah, a town in central Syria, from where, he sent secret agents calling for a rebellion against the Abbasid Caliphate.

He succeeded in his endeavour in the remote western provinces of the Abbasid Caliphate, away from the areas under the control of the Abbasid caliphs in the East, who were persecuting Shia Muslims. His agent, Abu Abdallah Al-Hussein, succeeded to reach a powerful position in the Aghlabid State of Ifriqia (present day Tunisia), from where he called Muhammad Al-Habib from Salamyah to head the new Fatimid Caliphate.

The Fatimid Caliphate covered large areas in North Africa and the Near East, as it extended from Morocco to Egypt alongside the Mediterranean coast, and was further extended by succeeding caliphs to include Sicily, the Hejaz in the Arabian Peninsula and Syria, and so became the biggest state opposing the Abbasid Caliphate of Baghdad, controlling the Holy sites in Hejaz and Palestine, and in a leadership position of Muslims. The Fatimids established their first capital – Al-Mahdia in the province of Ifriqia in AD 913, but when Jawhar Al-Siqilli, the army general of the third Fatimid Caliph Al-Mu'ez conquered Egypt in AD 969, the caliph moved to Egypt where he established his capital Al-Qahira (Cairo) to the north of Al-Fustat in AD 973. Egypt became the political, spiritual and cultural centre of the Fatimid Caliphate until its dissolution by Salah Al-Deen Al-Ayubi

(Saladin) in AD 1171 after the death of the last Fatimid caliph – Abu Muhammad Abdullah Al-Aded Lidin Illah.

Few Fatimid Caliphs tried to impose Ismaelite religious teachings onto their subjects, while most other Fatimid Caliphs were very tolerant towards the other Islamic sects, and also towards their Jewish and Christian subjects of different sects: Copts, Greeks, Syriacs and Maronites of Syria. They were reputed of being able to use the human resources of different ethnic components of their state: North African Berbers and Copts, Syrians, Turks, Ethiopians and Armenians besides Arabs.

The Ismaelite Sect absolutely negates any possibility to describe Allah, because they believe He is beyond the reach of Reason. He is the creator of the "First Reason" who alone owns the qualities of perfection, power, creation and life.

The Ismaelite theory of creation agrees, up to a certain degree with the Neo-Platonic philosophy of Plotinus (please refer to Chapter 3), whereby all creation radiates and proceeds from the "First Reason" (Hamid Al-Din Al-Karmani died around 1021 AD – *The Mind's Rest* كتاب راحة العقل pages 171–173).

The following are some of their beliefs:
-   The Koran is the first source of legislation, and contains levels of knowledge. For the simple reader, its verses have an apparent meaning but include a subtle esoteric meaning known only by the Ismaelite infallible Imams.
-   Numbers: each number has a meaning, for example: number seven.
-   The Imamate: It starts with Ali Ibn Abi-Taleb and is followed by his descendants. They believe that each epoch has its Imam who should have the

following qualities: Justice, courage, wisdom and honesty.

- The Apparent Meaning: The meaning of the Koran verses that is clear to anybody.

- The Batini Meaning: is the truth hidden behind the apparent meaning of the Koran and Scripture verses, known only by the infallible Ismaelite Imams.

- Reason: is the main legislation tool. If a Koran verse contradicts the requirements and challenges of the epoch, then the required legislation should be enacted without altering the spirit of the Koranic text.

- Imamate Governorship (Wilaya): Includes political and religious components. Muslims should obey the Imam if he is just, wise and honest, and should rebel and reject him if he is unjust, aggressive or defeatist. The Imam should keep peace and justice in society.

- The High Preacher: He is the intermediary between the Imam and his disciples. He passes unto them the Imams secret instructions and commands.

e. The Al-Muahhidoon also called "Druzes"
    The Al-Muahhidoon dislike to be called "Druzes" and insist on being called Al-Muahhidoon, which means: Those who believe in the "Oneness" of God. The name "Druze" was given to them by other Muslims based on a preacher by the name of Nashtakin Al-Durzi, whom they consider an alterer of truths and they dislike him.
    Al-Muahhidoon split from the Ismaelite Sect during the Fatimid caliphate in the tenth century, accordingly its origins are traced to Islamic roots, while from a

dogmatic religious point of view, some researchers do not consider this group a Muslim sect.

This religious group formed during the caliphate of Fatimid Caliph: Al-Hakem bi-Amr-Allah (AD 996–1021), who according to certain Islamic sources, requested from the Persian Ismaelite preacher: Hamza Ibn Ali to go to Syria to head the Ismaelite mission there. Hamza completed his mission successfully by spreading the Ismaelite teachings in certain areas of Syria and was rewarded by Caliph Al-Hakem the title: Al-Sañad Al-Hadi, meaning the Guiding Support. Hamza was assisted during his mission in Syria by an Ismaelite preacher named: Nashtakin Al-Durzi, who went to extremes by proclaiming Caliph Al-Hakem a manifestation of God on earth. Al-Durzi succeeded in proselytising a big number of people and taken by his success, gave himself the title: "The Leading Guide" and committed certain acts that angered some people and his boss Hamza.

News reached the Caliph, through Hamza about the preaching violations committed by Al-Durzi, and news of the Caliph's anger reached Al-Durzi. This prompted him and his supporter's to move to Cairo in AD 1018, surround the Ragdan mosque located close to the Caliph's palace where Hamza took refuge, force the mosque's door, and attempt to kill Hamza. The attackers didn't succeed and in the ensuing battle Al-Durzi was killed by Hamza.

On 23rd February AD 1021, Caliph Al-Hakem left his palace at night without guards, as was his habit and disappeared, prompting the Ismaelis in Cairo after waiting for his return over many days to declare his death, and named his son Al-Zaher Li-I'zaz-Din-Allah as the new Imam and Caliph of the Fatimid State. Hamza Ibn Ali refused to accept his death and announced that Imam Al-Hakem disappeared to reappear in a later day to fill planet Earth with Justice, in accordance with Shia beliefs. Since the disappearance of Al-Hakem, the "access door" to this religious group was closed by Hamza. The idea of the Imam's disappearance is common among the Twelve Imami and Alawite Muslim Shia Sects.

Al-Muahhidoon believe that there is no God but Allah, and that He is beyond the reach of our reason and beyond description. Certain orientalists reported about Al-muahhidoon's belief in the charter of the "World Governor" as the religion of the Oneness of God, and specifically recognize the imamate of Hamza and refuse all other religions and sects. The author of this charter is thought to be Hamza Ibn Ali. Al-Muahhidoon believe that this charter is eternal, that it incarnates the spirit of the "Al-Muahhid", as the Al-Muahhidoon believe in spirits incarnation. They also believe that whoever was admitted to the charter during Caliph Al-Hakem's earthly rule remains a Oneness believer in all his subsequent incarnations and lives.

Hamza Ibn Ali undertook on behalf of Imam Al-Hakem Bi-Amr-Allah to relieve his followers of the need of pilgrimage to Mecca, and Ramadan Fasting, and replaced them with the following commandments:

1. To tell the truth.
2. Take care of your brothers in Faith.
3. Reject the worship of idols and other gods.
4. Keep away from evils and injustice.
5. Believe in the Oneness of our Lord.
6. Accept our Lord acts for whatever happens.
7. Submit to the secret commands of our Lord.

The Muwahidoun marry from inside the sect, and marriage has to be based on acceptance, fairness and equality. That's why polygamy is forbidden, as they think it goes against fairness and equality. After marriage, the couple shall split equally their fortunes. Each of them has the right to ask for divorce.

The Muwahidoun recognise the Koran as a holy scripture. They base their beliefs on the "Wisdom Letters" composed by Hamza Ibn Ali, which are his interpretation of the Koran and the Scriptures. Access to the "Wisdom Letters" and other sacred books of the sect are forbidden to junior Al-Muwahhidoon sect followers (those below forty years), who might be gradually initiated to them after reaching the age of forty, if they are of high ethical standing and persons of confidence. Their sacred scriptures are kept by some highly positioned "Sheikhs Al-Akl" (clerics).

6. H. 2 The Philosophical current in Islam

a. Al-Mu'tazila school of thought

The Al-Mu'tazila group is one of the most important Muslim religious groups that appeared in Basra, Iraq, at the end of the Omayyad Caliphate, and blossomed during the Abbasid Age. It based its beliefs on reason, and said that by using reason a person could differentiate between bad and good without relying on the Koranic text. Among the renowned Mutazila intellectuals were: Caliph Al-Ma'moun (الخليفة العالم المأمون) and writer/philosopher Al-Jahez (الجاحظ), Abu Al-Hudail – the Basra School, Al-Nazzam, and Abu Yousef Al-Kindi.

The cause for the appearance of this religious group are historical and cultural, as the Arab Muslim State has expanded over a short period of time over many countries, and many peoples with their civilizations, cultures and religious beliefs became part of this new society, and contacts between all its components multiplied. Greek Philosophical thinking, especially Neo Platonism caught the attention of Muslim intellectuals, and the more conventional Arab Muslim way of thinking relying on a literal (word for word) interpretation of the Koran couldn't satisfy them anymore. The Mu'tazila was the Muslim Sect most attached to reason.

The Mu'tazila reliance on the idea of the Oneness of God, reason and social justice, among others, lead to the spread of their ideas to many provinces of the Muslim Caliphate: in Khorasan, Yemen and Kufa besides the capital Bagdad.

The Mu'tazila Sect met a formidable resistance in the final years of the Abbasid Caliphate from conservative Salafi Muslim scholars, resulting in the intentional destruction and loss of most of this religious school literature over the centuries. Recently, a book covering Al-Mu'tazila's teachings was found in Yemen under the title "المغني في أبواب التوحيد والعدل" collected by Kadi: Abdel Jabbar.

From what was assembled from different sources, the Mu'tazila beliefs could be resumed as follows:

1. The belief in the Oneness of God.

   They declared that it is impossible to describe God, and that He does not resemble anything material we know, and that no resemblance exists between God and all His creatures.

2. God's Justice

   That His commandments are based on reason, wisdom and justice, accordingly, they denied that God can be the creator of the deeds of humans and said that humans are the creators of their deeds, either good or bad.

   That all deeds of humans in their sayings and actions are not created by the All-Merciful God. That God can only do and guide to good deeds, in opposition to the "Jabria" Muslim Sect who based their beliefs on certain verses of the Koran to show that human deeds are created by God and that man cannot control his fate.

   They said also that using reason, a person could differentiate between good and bad, in opposition to the Salafist School who relied on the Koranic text to find if deeds are good or bad.

3. They also declared that an evil-doer cannot be called either a believer, or an unbeliever.

   If he repents – he will be saved, but if he dies insistent on his misdeeds, hell is his fate.

4. God's Punishment

   The Mutazila believed that if a Muslim dies truly repentant, God will accept his repentance.

5. "Invite to goodness and forbid indecency" (Verse 104 Surah 3).

   Imam Al-Ash'ari in his book *Al-Maqalat* "المقالات" said that the Mutazila required from Muslims, apart from the deaf, to "Invite to goodness, and enjoin right conduct and forbid indecency" as much as possible, by mouth and hand and if required by the sword, and that they made it a duty for Muslims to fight unjust and impious Imams.

6. That God cannot be seen in this world nor in the next (as per certain verses of the Koran), because by seeing Him, we can determine his location, but God does not have a known location and no direction could lead to Him. That the verse 22–23 of Surah 75: "That day, faces will be resplendent. Looking toward their Lord" should be understood by making the word "toward" to mean "the grace of", because if we can see God, then God becomes a material being.

7. They declared that the Koran was created. They said that God spoke to Prophet Moses from a shrub (tree), which means that His speech was created after not been in existence. Abbasid Caliph Al-Ma'moun commanded Muslim scholars to admit the creation of the Koran.

8. They negate that God is sitting on a throne, as per (verse 5 of Surah 20: "The Beneficent One, established on the Throne.")

9. They negate the intercession of Prophet Muhammad with God for Muslim sinners.

10. They negate the intercession of Muslim saints with God.

b. The Muslim Philosophers

During the end days of the Abbasid Caliphate, provoked by the weakening political and military powers of the Caliph, the caliphate broke down to several states and many Muslim sects made their appearance. A number of intellectuals emerged amongst whom are:

Abou Bakr Al-Razi (AD 865-923):

A famous medical doctor and philosopher of Persian origin, who believed that the aim of people in this life, shall be the pursuit of happiness. He found that religions and religious sects with their beliefs based on subjective assumptions, their disputes and fights didn't bring to mankind harmony, understanding and peace, but hatred, retribution and wars. He called for a return to the old Greek Philosophers teachings, especially Socrates, Plato and Aristotle, as he found they served humanity better.

He wrote several books amongst whom are: *The Philosophical History* "السيرة الفلسفية", *Al-Mansoury in Medicine* "المنصوري في الطب" and *The spiritual Medicine* "الطب الروحاني". In the first chapter of that last book, He wrote about the merit of reason: "... we should not make it ruled while it is the ruler, and not to depreciate it while it is the all precious, and not to make it a follower while it is a leader, but to refer to it in all our judgments...". He believed that progress in medical studies couldn't be achieved without the study of the achievements of the previous generations of medical physicians. So in his book *Al-Mansoury in Medicine* he wrote: "This industry will not allow a single person to achieve much, if he does not base his search on what the previous generations have accomplished, even if he spends all his life on it, because its perfection is much longer than the life span of a single person, and not only this industry but most other industries as well...".

Abou Nasr Muhammad Al-Farabi (AD 874–950):

Born in Khoarezm of Turkish parents, he spent the last part of his life at the court of Saif Al-Daoula Al-Hamadani in Aleppo.

He tried to accommodate the Koran's Sharia with philosophical thought, especially Neo-Platonism, and the principle of the "the overflow of power by the One" "نظريّة الفيض". He spoke about the resurrection of the spirit after death, but not the material body, and limited the resurrection to knowledgeable spirits and not to ignorant ones.

The most important part in his philosophy dealt with politics that he based on Plato's "Republic" and "The Law".

Abou Ali Al-Hussein Ibn Sina (Avicenna AD 980–1037):

Most famous medical physician and Muslim philosopher, of Persian origin, lived during the rule of the Boweihid Shia dynasty. He was influenced by the translated works of Greek Philosophers Plato and Aristotle and was the one who established the philosophical current that challenged the prophetical idea in Islam and the mission of Prophet Muhammad. He said that the world was ancient and negated God's creation of the world, as well as the resurrection of the body. Of his philosophical works the book: *Al-Isharat* "كتاب الإشارات".

His companionship of certain gnostic (Batini) interpreters/philosophers of the Koran, including Abou Abdallah Al-Nae'li, led him to search for a reasonable interpretation of the Koran, which made him think that philosophers are equal to the prophets, as he wrote in his book: *The Theory of Knowledge* "نظرية المعرفة". He distinguished philosophers by saying that they are continuing their mission leading toward the progress of humanity, while the mission of prophets ended with Prophet Muhammad.

Ibn Rushd (Averroes AD 1126–1298):

A Muslim jurist, philosopher and medical doctor born in Al-Andalus (Spain). He studied the jurisprudence of Al-Maliki School and Al-Sharia of Al-Ash'ari School. He defended philosophy and tried to correct the beliefs of certain Muslim philosophers as Al-Farabi and Ibn Sina who were influenced by Plato and Aristotle, and saw that there was no contradiction between philosophy and religion and tried to find a compromise between them. He expressed his opposition to Al-Ghazali, who called Al-Farabi and Ibn Sina unbelievers (Kafir), explained in two main books: *Clarification of the Relationship Between Wisdom and Sharia* "فصل المقال فيما بين الحكمة والشريعة من الاتصال" and *Downfall of the Downfall* "تهافت التهافت". He was accused at the end of his life of atheism and unbelief by some extremist Muslim faqihs.

He believed in the eternity of the material world, and declared that the spirit is divided into two parts: one part belongs to man and the other to God. He wrote about two ways to reach the truth, the first based on religion for the simple-minded people, that cannot be submitted to the rule of reason and logic, and the second is the philosophic way to reach the truth that only few intellectuals master.

6. H. 3. The Sunni Muslims Schools

These are Muslims who believe that the Koran is Allah's Book, revealed literally (word by word) to Prophet Muhammad, and believe in its apparent meaning. They also believe in Prophet Muhammad's Al-Hadith (talk/speech), his life example (Sunnah) and the Muslim Nation's consensus.

Their belief in Al-Hadith and the Prophet's Sunnah is what differentiates them from Shia Muslims, and other sects that discard the Al-Hadith as being altered, being transmitted orally by generations of people over time, while the Shia Imams interpret the Koran using reason and purpose, and believe that the highest elected Imam unifies in his person political and religious leadership of Muslims, and is the only one with the authority to interpret the Koranic text.

The admiration towards Prophet Muhammad's life example (he was a politician, warlord and statesman besides being a prophet), and the separation of the religious Imamate from the political leadership that started by the Omayyad Caliphs, after establishing their capital in Damascus, the provincial capital of Byzantine Syria similar to the roles of the Byzantine Emperor and the Patriarch of Constantinople, gave to Sunni Muslims a more prominent historical and geopolitical role in shaping events than Shia Muslims. Sunni Muslims rely on the example of the Prophet in his military campaigns and tactical political alliances during his life to give a more prominent political and military role to the Caliph, leaving the discussion of religious matters and the interpretation of the Koran's Sharia and Al-Hadith in the hands of Muslim imams and scholars, while keeping the final decision to the Caliph.

The Muslim Sunni schools of teaching started in fact during the days of the Omayyad Caliphate, at the hands of Imam Abou Hanifa Al-Numaan Ibn Thabet and Imam Malek Ibn Anas, who lived most of their lives during that caliphate. That Caliphate witnessed important changes entered in government rule (the monarchic dynastic rule), and changes in the way of life of

Muslim Arabs after their contact with the culture of conquered peoples. The Sunni schools of teaching continued their development under the Abbasid Caliphate by Imam Muhammad Ibn Idriss Al-Shafee and Imam Ahmad Ibn Hanbal, this later being the unwavering opponent of the Shia sects and the Mutazila Philosophic School, supported by the Abbasid Caliph Al-Mutawakil Ala-Allah.

Imam Abou Hanifa Al-Numaan Ibn Thabet (died AD 773)

Was one of the jurisprudence teachers at the Opinion School (Al-Rai school) in Kufa. It was reported that he was not an opponent to the teachings of Shia Imam Jaafar Al-Sadeq. Al-Shahrastani said that Abou Hanifa didn't hide his sympathy and attachment to the house of the Prophet, and his respect to Imams Ali, Al-Hasan and Al-Hussein, Ali Ibn Al-Hussein, Zeid Ibn Ali and Muhammad Ibn Abdallah.

In his book: *Al-Fiqh Al-Akbar* "الفقه الأكبر", Abou Hanifa criticized the divisions introduced by the Khawarej and Al-Kadaria sects, but his criticism of Shia sects was more moderate. He didn't criticize Caliph Othman and Caliph Ali and adopted the point of view of Al-Murjia Sect towards them. In general, his attitude in beliefs was closer to Al-Murjia, i.e.: we cannot accuse a Muslim of unbelief (Kufr) due to his actions. That Allah will judge the companions of the Prophet the day of Resurrection due to their disputes covering the Caliph election. Several sources mention Abou Hanifa's recommendation to check the reliability of the Prophet's Al-Hadith, and to accept some as true only after a careful investigation.

Imam Malek Ibn Anas (died AD 795)

Imam Malek spent most of his life in Medina – Hejaz. He established the second in its importance Sunni jurisprudence school after that of Abou Hanifa, and is considered one of the main establishers of Al-Hadith School. His book: *Al Maoute'* "الموطأ" is a study of Islamic Jurisprudence "Fiqh" based mainly on the Prophet's Al-Hadith taken from Medinan sources, especially Abdallah ibn Omar Ibn Al-Khattab (the son of the second caliph) and to a lesser extent: Abdallah Ibn Al-Abbas and Ali Ibn Abi Taleb. Maleq called for the use of logic and purpose to differentiate between the correct and fake Al-Hadith.

He didn't take sides in the dispute between Othman and Ali and confirmed the legality of both of them for eligibility to the caliphate. He severely criticized the Qadaria Sect that based its teachings on the apparent meaning of certain verses of the Koran. Imam Malek said that if a person believed that his fate is already written and he cannot change it, such belief could lead to corruption in society. He demanded the state to fight the extremist sect of Al-Khawarej.

Imam Al-Shafe'ee (died AD 820)

Imam Al-Shafe'ee was born in Gaza – Palestine and spent most of his life during the Abbasid Caliphate. He received his teaching in Mecca by the Salafist: Muslim ibn Khaled Al-Zinj and in Medina by Imam Malek Ibn Anas. He defended Malek's classification of Al-Hadith to correct and weak. His school is considered to represent the Salafist School based on the Koran and the Al-Hadith.

In his book: *Letter about the origins of Fiqh* "الرسالة في أصول الفقه" he explained the contribution of each of the following sources: the Koran, the Al-Hadith and the Analogy in forming the Consensus of Muslims. It seems that he tried to find a compromise between the teachings of different Muslim jurisprudence schools.

Imam Ahmad Ibn Hanbal (died AD 855)

Was born in Baghdad and was a fervent supporter of Al-Hadith School. He lived in a period when the teaching of Greek Philosophers and the civilizations of the conquered peoples (Persians, Greeks, Syrians, Egyptians...) have altered the ways of thinking and life of the conquering Arabs, events that lead to the appearance of many Islamic sects, some of which tried to reconcile philosophic thought with religion. One of the most famous of these religious groups was the Mu'tazila Philosophic School, supported as mentioned above by Caliph Al-Ma'moun and writer/philosopher Al-Jahez. After the advent of Abbasid Caliph Al-Mutawakil, Imam Ahmad Ibn Hanbal found in the person of the new Caliph a strong supporter in his fight against the Shia and other sects that do not base their teaching on Al-Hadith, the most prominent amongst them was Al-Mu'tazila group.

One of the most important of his books is: *Al-Musnad* "المُسند", where he classified the Al-Hadith based on the reliability of the person who relayed it. He tried to assemble all the Al-Hadith known in those days. Another of his books is: *Osool Al-Sunnah* "أصول السنة" where he criticized the Jahmiah and Murjiaa Sects. His books include also *Al-Wara* "الورع" and *Al-Zuhd* "الزهد".

Ahmad Ibn Hanbal closed with his teachings and thinking the Sunni Jurisprudence School, especially in what relates to Al-Hadith. In his writings, he stressed the necessity to believe in Allah as Allah described Himself in the Koran, and as taught in Al-Hadith by Prophet Muhammad. He concentrated on both Allah's Spiritual and Material qualities, and that the Koran is not created and that it contains the exact words of Allah. He confirmed the necessity to respect the four first caliphs and the Omayyad Caliph Mu'awia. He fiercely attacked the other sects, especially Al-Khawarej and all Shia sects (Twelve Imami, Zeidi, Gnostic Muslim groups "الفرق الباطنة"), and also Al-Jahmia, Al-Murjia and Al-Mutazila.

Imam Abou Hamed Muhammad Al-Ghazali (AD 1058-1111)

Imam Al-Ghazali was a Sunni Faqih born in the town of Tous (Persia). He went to Baghdad as a teacher in Al-Nizamieh School at the demand of the Turkish Seljuk minister Nizam Al-Mulk, during the Abbasid Caliphate disintegration period.

He was a follower of the Shafe'e Jurisprudence School, and Soufi in his approach to worship.

He criticized Ali Ibn Sina in his books Tahafut Al-Falasifa "تهافت الفلاسفة" and *Al-Munqez min Al-Dalal* "المنقذ من الضلال", where in that last book he accused Ibn Sina of unbelief (Kufr) and wrote: "We should accuse them of unbelief and condemn their philosophical sects, the likes of Ibn Sina, Al-Farabi, and others". He condemned Ibn Sina because of his belief in the ancienty (continuous existence) of the world, his negation of resurrection and his saying that Allah does not know the details.

As Philosophy during the life of Al-Ghazali had affected the minds of many people, Al-Ghazali counterattacked by writing his book: *Maqased Alfalasifah* "مقاصد الفلاسفة" where he exposed their approach and concluded saying: "I classified them in categories, and divided their studies according to subjects, but all of them deserve to be qualified as disbelievers and atheists, even though there is a huge difference amongst some of the ancient and some of the recent ones, regarding the distance of each of them from the Truth".

Al-Ghazali studied the philosophical works of ancient Greek Philosophers as well as the works of his Muslim contemporaries in an analytical way, and was considered the first Muslim scholar to conduct such a methodical analysis and the first to classify their philosophical works and to acknowledge the correctness of some of them. His critique of philosophers was related to their problematic belief in God, as that was where they made, according to him, most mistakes. It was said that, by his works, he destroyed the philosophical thinking based on reason in Muslim countries for many centuries, until Ibn Rushd came to answer him with two of his books: *Fasl Al-Maqal fima bayn Al-Hikma wal Sharia min Ittisal* "فصل المقال فيما بين الحكمة والشريعة من الاتصال" and *tahafut al-tahafut* "تهافت التهافت".

Many Muslim scholars believe that in spite of Al-Ghazali's attacks against Muslim Philosophical thinking, he was influenced by it.

Ahmad Ibn Abdel-Haleem Ibn Taymieh (AD 1263-1330):

Ahmad Ibn Taymieh is one of the extremist faqihs of the Hanbali Jurisprudence School, lived during the rule of the Mameluke Sultans over Egypt and Syria. He was born in Harran, in Northern Mesopotamia.

When the Mongols invaded Harran, he and his family moved to Damascus, where he grew up and was taught by his father and the faqihs of that epoch. His fame in interpreting Al-Hadith was great regarding his approach in resolving the conflict between the circulating many copies of Al-Hadith and logical thinking. It was said that he recommended Jihad (holy war) against infidels and the strict application of Sharia Law. He was influential in the growth of the political current in Islam.

Many Maliki and Shafe'ee scholars of his time criticized him believing that he went against the Muslims consensus that included: the prevention of Muslims from visiting the tombs of saints and prophets, the interceding of Muslim saints with Allah, certain subjects related to divorce, his unorthodox ways of interpreting Al-Hadith and others. It pushed them to complain to the Mameluke Sultan who forced Ibn Taymieh to travel to Egypt to discuss his views. After discussions with Egypt's Muslim scholars and its jurisprudence judges, he was found guilty of heresy and was jailed twice. He returned to Damascus later where he caused the Damascene faqihs after further disputes to ask the Damascus governor to jail him, and was released later at the request of Sultan Qalaoun. He continued to teach, was jailed again and continued writing up to his death in the Damascus citadel prison. He wrote many books including: "فتاوى ابن تيمية, الجمع بين العقل والنقل, منهاج السنّة النبوية في نقض الشيعة والقدرية". Some view him as a Muslim renovator in his days.

The late Abbasid caliphs as well as the Ayoubite Sultans (especially Nour Al-Din Zanki), the Mameluke Sultans, and the Turkish Ottoman Sultans based their jurisprudence laws on the four Sunni jurisprudence schools: Hanafi, Maliki, Shafe'ee and Hanbali. Sunni Muslims constitute about 88% of the total Muslim population of the world at present.

6.H. 4. The Al-Murjia Sect

The Al-Murjia Sect is an Islamic group that disagreed with the Al-Khawarej Sect but also with the Sunni Sect regarding the judgment of whoever commits a grave sin and other dogmatic matters. They declared that whoever believes in the Oneness of Allah cannot be judged as unbeliever, as his judgment befalls to the Almighty and Just Allah the day of Resurrection, whatever are the sins he committed.

Their opinion is not to condemn as unbeliever (Kafir) any Muslim who confess that: "there is only One God and that Muhammad is his messenger". While in the Al-Khawarej view, for example, the grave sinner is considered a unbeliever and his fate is hell.

6.H. 5. The Wahhabi Sect

It is a radical Muslim movement, of tribal character, that started in the remote, sparsely populated region of Najd in the Arabian Peninsula during the eighteenth century by a Muslim preacher and activist named Muhammad Ibn Abdel Wahhab (AD 1703-1792) advocating a purge of certain widespread Sunni practices. He formed a pact with a local leader: Muhammad Ibn Saud offering political obedience and the later promising protection. He started in Al-Dar'ea where Muhammad Ibn Abdel Wahhab declared the Jihad (Ibn Bushr, *Glorious Pages in the History of Najd,* pages 45–53) by starting a series of raids in the Arabian Peninsula killing a number of his Muslim enemies and plundering their wealth, with the stated goal of establishing a true faith Muslim state based on the good practices of the Prophet and his companions "the good salaf", to purify the Muslim faith from idolatry (*shirk*), impurities and innovations in Islam (Bid'ah) and superstitions. His actions provoked many Muslim scholars and faqihs to call him "Khawarej" (religious outlaw), because the Wahhabis applied the Koran verses regarding retribution towards infidels against their fellow Muslims (Yousef Al-Refaee: a counsel to our brothers – the scholars in Najd page 17). Meanwhile the Wahhabis believe that they are the only true Muslims, and are the only Muslim group to be saved from hell.

The result of these raids was the establishment of the first Wahabi State in parts of Najd and surrounding areas in AD 1786. On 21st April 1802, the Wahabi combatants attacked the town of Karbala in Iraq and pillaged and destroyed the mausoleum of Imam Al-Hussein, the grandson of Prophet Muhammad and the most important place of worship for Shia Muslims. At the request of the Ottoman Sultan, Muhammad Ali – the Pasha of Egypt sent a military expedition headed by his son Ibrahim in AD 1818 to fight the Wahhabi Sect in Najd, resulting in the siege of their capital Al-Dar'ea and its destruction. Later the Wahhabis rose again and established in the early years of the twentieth century under the protection of Abdel Aziz Ibn Saud (AD 1902–53) the Kingdom of Saudi Arabia.

The Wahhabi movement preached the Salafist way (Prophet Muhammad's and his companions approach) in what it considered a way to purify the beliefs of Muslims from certain practices that spread later in Muslim countries, that the Wahhabis consider contradictory to the essence of the Muslim faith: like the supplications and calls for blessing to Muslim saints, pilgrimage to the tombs of these saints, music, representations of any live creature, photography and in general any heresies that contradict the Koran's Sharia, the way of life and approach of Prophet Muhammad, his companions and the Muslim ancestors approach against unbelievers. That meant also that practically, there was no strong need to follow the interpretation of the four jurisprudence Sunni Schools, as long as a Muslim person follows literally the apparent meaning of the Koran's Sharia and the correct Al-Hadith (according to Imam Ahmad Ibn Hanbal) and condemns as unbelief (Kufr) whatever teaching contradicts these holy texts. In this last category are included the interpretations of the Shia Imams, all the gnostic interpretations of Muslim sects: Alawite, Ismaeli. Druze, Zaidi, Mu'tazila, all Soufi sects and also some Sunni innovators like Al-Ghazali, Abu Mansour Al-Baghdadi or Fakhr Eldin Al-Razi.

Muhammad Ibn Abdel Wahhab based his beliefs on those of Ibn Taymieh in regard to Muslim Fiqh (jurisprudence), the purification of the Muslim faith and the literal execution of Muslim Sharia laws. The Wahhabis adopted the idea of a religious state based on Muslim Sharia. For a long time, Ibn Abd Al-Wahhab's teachings were the official, form of Islam in Saudi Arabia.

Saudi Arabia until recently was applying the Wahabi Sect principles using a committee called: "Invite to goodness and forbid indecency" " هيئة الأمر بالمعروف والنهي عن المنكر ". The committee's employees swept the streets of Saudi towns and imposed on people practices (regarding clothing, drinking, prayer time, women waking without a male legal attendant, cars driven by women...) that are considered in other Muslim countries a personal choice. The Wahhabis destroyed what remaining buildings were standing of the birthplace of Prophet Muhammad, his house in Mecca, the houses and tombs of his relatives and companions.

The majority of Sunni and Shia Muslims worldwide disagree with Wahhabi teachings, and many Muslims denounce them as a vile sect. Wahhabism has been accused of being a source of global terrorism, inspiring the ideology of Al-Qaeda, the Islamic State of Iraq and the Levant (ISIL), the Somali Al-Shabab, Boko Haram and others.

Syria, Palmyra Temple of Baal, 1st Century AD, dedicated to the Aramean god Baal before destruction by ISIS (Islamic State of Iraq & Syria)

Syria, Palmyra Temple of Baal, 1st Century AD, windows detail

Syria, Palmyra Temple of Baal, 1st Century AD, after complete destruction by ISIS in August 2015

Syria, Palmyra Roman Theatre 2nd Century AD before destruction by ISIS.

Syria, Palmyra Roman Theatre 2nd Century AD after the façade destruction by ISIS.

Syria, Palmyra Temple of Baal Shammin, 2nd Century AD, dedicated to the Aramean sky deity, before complete destruction by ISIS in 2015

Syria, Palmyra Tower Tomb of Lamblichus, 1st Century AD, before complete destruction by ISIS. Other tower tombs, including the admirably preserved Tower Tomb of Elahbaal, were destroyed by ISIS as well

Syria, Deir Ez Zor, Syrian Orthodox Church of the Virgin Mary after destruction by An-Nusra (Al-Qaeda) bomb in 2012. This church is one of tens of Christian Churches destroyed in Syria and Iraq by ISIS and its Al-Qaeda sisters.

One of many buildings destroyed in Aleppo Syria during the civil war 2013-2018

6. H. 6. The Soufi Sects

The Soufi movement started in the tenth century during the end days of the Abbasid Caliphate, after the demise of the Mu'tazila movement, as an individual approach to God's worship, striving to abstain from the delights of terrestrial life. It developed later and became known as the Soufi ways of worship. Islamic history is full of Muslim scholars who joined the Soufi approach in worship as Shams Al-Tabrizi, Jalal Al-din Al-Roumi, Imam Al-Naouaoui, Imam Abu Hamid Al-Ghazali, but also military/political leaders as Salah Al-Din Al-Ayoubi (Saladin) and Abdel Qader Al-Jazaeri.

As many simple-minded people entered the Soufi movement, it became exposed to certain mistaken practices over the centuries. These practices were attacked especially by the followers of the Salafist School who considered them heresies to the true Muslim faith. The Soufis concentrated on developing ways of worship in order to get a better knowledge of Allah and get closer to Him, and to follow his commandments regarding ethical ways of behaviour. They based their approach on both the Koran and Al-Hadith, and made their movement into a specific school with its imams and teachers who wrote many books exposing their ideas, as: *Al-Hikam Al-Ata'iah* by Imam Ibn Ataa Allah Al-Iskandari, and the: *Al-Risala Al-Qushairiah* by Imam Al-Qushairi, and others.

The methods of worship and personal discipline used by the Sheikhs (leaders) of this sect differ greatly. Some Sheikhs might follow very strict methods forcing their followers to many days of fasting, prayers and seclusion while others use milder methods. Accordingly they say: Allah has worship approaches as variable as the number of His creations.

6. H. 7. The Khawarej Sect

They are a group of Muslims that opposed the decision of Caliph Ali Ibn Abi Taleb for arbitration in the aftermath of the battle of Saffin saying: "There is no judge but Allah". After the destitution of Caliph Ali that resulted from his acceptance of arbitration, their certainty increased about the correctness of their attitude and requested Caliph Ali to refuse the results of the arbitration and to continue the fight against Mu'awia, but he answered saying: "Could we repudiate it after we signed it, that's not correct. (*Al-Tabari* Vol. 1 pages 334–336)". Here, the Khawarej definitively split from the followers of Ali and accused him of unbelief (Kufr) and called themselves: "The Believing Group", while their opponents called them: "Khawarej".

The Khawarej do not pose as a precondition for a Muslim belonging to any race, colour and parentage, to become Imam or Caliph. That's what explains the entry of many conquered Persians and North African Berbers into this sect later. They declared that Muslims should rise against the injustice, impiety and weaknesses of Imams and Caliphs. The Khawarej accept the election of Abou Bakr Al-Sidiq, Omar Ibn Al-Khattab and Othman Ibn Affan to the Caliphate for only the period preceeding the last six years of the later's caliphate. Regarding Caliph Ali Ibn Abi Taleb, they count him an unbeliever after his acceptance of arbitration. Al-Khawarej believe that Caliphs should be freely elected, and refuse the opinion of those who believe that the imamate shall be hereditary in the dynasty of Prophet Muhammad.

They believe that Allah is Just and Merciful, therefore He cannot be the One who determines man's fate, and that men are free to decide and choose their deeds and actions. They also believe that Allah does not resemble any of his creatures.

Chapter seven

Is peaceful coexistence possible between Christianity and Islam?

As we mentioned in chapters two, five and six, there are many similarities between the Torah, and the Koran. Many verses in the Koran, especially those related to the Sharia, bear big resemblance to those of Moses' Law, with some few and small differences. Regarding food, clothing, prayers, ablutions, fasting and the First Qibla, but also the Sharia Limits (penalties) and slavery, we find many similarities, and to a lesser extent regarding marriage and inheritance. This resemblance should not surprise us, as Prophet Muhammad was acquainted with the Bible due to his contacts with the Christian Clergy and the Jewish Rabbis. As we mentioned in Chapter 6 C, the uncle of Khadija – his first wife, Waraka Ibn Naoufal, was a Christian priest in Mecca. Also during his travels to the town of Bosra in Southern Syria, he met the Christian Arian monk Bahira as mentioned in Chapter 6 C, and subsequently after his migration to Yathrib had met and corresponded with the Jewish Rabbis as reported by Zaid Ibn Thabet Al-Ansari in Chapter 6 F.

Prophet Muhammad with his logical analytical mind listened and discussed the different interpretations of the Evangels with Christians of different sects and later discussed the Torah with Jewish Rabbis in Yathrib, and came to appreciate the Torah that contained the Law of Moses which dealt with religious and socio-economic problems similar to those of his tribal people, and reached certain conclusions that he tried to express in a book "revealed" to him in Arabic language where he tried to correct the misinterpretations of the Bible by others, and to serve as a guide for his people, where he used the Torah's Moses' Law to generate a similar Arabic Sharia Law – a solid legislative basis for the establishment of an Arab Muslim State.

Let us also not forget that the Nasara of the Koran (Arian Christians) that he met in Mecca and elsewhere were also followers of Moses' Law.

Another common feature between Judaism and Islam is God's (Allah's) command to both Israelis and Muslims to fight His and their enemies: For the Israelis – their ethnic enemies in the Land of Canaan (Deuteronomy 20: 16–17) and for Muslims – their religious enemies (Verse 29 Surah 9 and many others). God instructed both on how to deal with their enemies after they subjugate them (Deuteronomy 20: 10–14 for the Israelis) and (Verse 65, 67 & 69 of Surah 8, Verse 20 of Surah 48 and others for the Muslims). Also for both, God affirmed that they are His chosen people (Deuteronomy 14: 2 for the Israeli People) and (Verse 110 of Surah 3 for the Muslim Nation).

An in-depth reading of the Bible and the Koran reveals the difference in Prophet Muhammad's beliefs before the death of his first wife Khadija and her uncle the Christian priest Waraka, when he followed the Christian teaching in peacefully calling for the belief in a Merciful and Omnipotent Single God, and was oppressed because of it, lead a monogamous life, and after her death and the death of Christian priest Waraka and his migration to Yathrib, where he had as neighbours the Jewish Rabbis.

After his migration to Yathrib, his approach in calling for the worship of a single God changed. Gone were his peaceful ways, and we start finding a big similarity between the lifestyle of Prophet Muhammad and the Israeli Prophets/Kings David and Solomon: Both were rulers besides being prophets and the establishers of earthly states. Their constitution was that of the Law of Moses. They lead Israel's wars against their enemies (and God's enemies) to expand the Land of Israel, married many women, had many slaves and concubines and fathered many sons. The terrestrial state established by Prophet Muhammad after his migration to Yathrib (Medina) and the Sharia Law of the Koran resembles in many aspects these Hebrew states ruled by these prophets/kings, and is in sharp contrast with the Heavenly Kingdom preached by Jesus Christ described in Chapter 5.

This similarity between Prophet Muhammad and Israel's prophets/kings, was probably due to his belief that he shared the same ancestry with the Israeli prophets, this time through the lineage of Ishmael son of Abraham, the lineage that brought to the world some Ishmaelite prophets (mentioned in the Koran but not in the Bible) like Prophets Saleh, Hood and Shuaib, although in the case of Prophet Muhammad, he came about one thousand five hundred years after prophets/kings David and Solomon. Therefore, he felt the need to take into account the religious, social, and scientific developments that took place during that long period of time, in the formulation of the new Muslim State's constitution (Sharia Law), modifications to the Law of Moses that would take into account the Jewish prophets/kings failure to establish a durable earthly state, as Moses' Law was destined to be a state constitution for the Israelite People only. Also, another "weak" point in the Torah, according to Muhammad, was that it didn't indulge sufficiently to describe the torture endured in hell by sinners, and the rewards in Paradise to befall the good. After his move to Yathrib (Medina), he somehow discarded the teaching of Jesus, son of Mary – the Messiah, who abrogated the strict punishments and other rules of Moses' Law and came with his mission of love, tolerance and God's promise of redemption from Adam's original sin to humankind, opening the way for a Heavenly Kingdom, just judgement and eternal life (Matthew 5: 3–10).

In spite of the "improvements" entered into the Koran's Sharia, the Sharia remains a tribal constitution that appropriated much of its components from Moses' Law. The state and its legislation established in the seventh century by Prophet Muhammad was also, that for a tribal society in a country outside the borders of the Roman Empire. The Koran's Sharia is still thought by many Muslims in our present day, to be God's Law applicable by societies living in any country and at any time. It might have allowed the expansion of the early Muslim Arab State during a certain period in history, and the amalgam of the cultures of many peoples that it subjugated into an Islamic culture, but as we know, any sound constitution cannot freeze in time, and should take into account the development of society from many aspects: social, economical, technical and scientific.

Most of the scientific knowledge (astronomical, geographical, mathematical, architectural, medical) in that age developed outside the Arabian Peninsula. The *Almagest* book of Ptolemy – a Greek geographer and astronomer – who lived in Alexandria, Egypt in the second century AD, taught that the Earth is a sphere and that it is at the centre of the universe. That the Moon, Mercury, Venus, Sun, Mars, Jupiter, Saturn rotated around it in that sequence, proportional to their distance from the Earth, and that each of them is moving in its own heaven, i.e. there were seven heavens. Also in his book *Geography*, Ptolemy fixed the coordinates of the then known countries by their coordinates, having divided the Earth's sphere into latitude lines starting from the Equator, and longitude lines starting from the western coast of Africa (Longitude 0°) and ending in the eastern most country known then: China (Longitude 180°), with the description of each country.

In Medical sciences, the Greek medical doctor and surgeon Galen who lived also in the second century AD wrote about the anatomy of the human body, physiology, pathology and pharmacology; their writings were known by certain intellectuals in Syria and Egypt, mostly by Christian monks. That's what we find in the Koran when we read about the existence of seven heavens (Verse 44 of Surah 17) and Prophet Muhammad's request to Muslims to learn sciences even if they have to travel to China, the farthest country in the world (Hadith).

It shows the interest of Prophet Muhammad and his contacts (Greek and Syrian Christian monks, Jewish Rabbis and other intellectuals) in the sciences of his epoch and deserves praise for having incorporated in the Koran some scientific knowledge of his time (with all its deficiencies as we know at present).

Even if the ideas in the Bible and the Koran were inspired by God, the tools who transmitted them to mankind were human, using the reasoning and language expression capabilities of human imperfect persons in the form of words and their language proficiency, but also the level of their scientific knowledge and the traditions of their societies.

These revelations were also written with the level of writing skills of their time, as the art of writing and copying was at its beginning. The number of people who could read and write in Arabia was very limited (could be counted on the fingers of a single hand) and the scriptures were written many years after the death of Moses, resurrection of Jesus and the death of Mohammed (tens and hundreds of years), from the memories of the Hebrew rabbis, disciples of Christ and the companions of Prophet Muhammad, and all of us know the deficiencies of memory.

Although Semitic languages were the first in history to be written with alphabetical letters, the techniques used to write them were still primitive. For example the Aramaic, Hebrew and the Arabic alphabets didn't include vowels, and the Koran, which was written in New Syriac Arabic (Old Kufi) alphabet in the seventh century AD didn't include vowels and articulations (points and accents), as these were added much later.

I refer here to the fourteenth century renowned Muslim historian Ibn Khaldoun in his *Introduction Book* (Chapter 30:"… Arabic writing skills at the beginning of Islam were not of good quality, as the Arabs were backward nomads distant from civilization. Look what happened when they wrote the Koran, as it was drawn by the Prophet companions with their incapable hands…").

Copying the scriptures was done by hand as the art of printing was not yet invented, and by hand copying these scriptures during centuries by a multitude of scribes, many mistakes must have occurred. Mistakes also could have occurred while translating from one language to another.

I am not mentioning here the fact that some scribes might have added or deleted certain words, or complete verses.

The revelations to the prophets of the Old Testament and to Prophet Muhammad, are not different from inspirations to Socrates, Plato, Aristotle and Plotinus who all tried using the reason given to them by God to find Him (see Chapter 3).

Socrates came to believe in an Eternal Soul, full of all knowledge. He taught that there are two worlds: a visible world of ever-changing phenomena and another one invisible and unchanging which controls the visible changing one. He emphasized the existence of an Absolute Justice in the world. Plato identifies the ideal with God who is perfect goodness. God created the world out of matter and shaped it according to his ideal. The body is material and mortal, and the soul is ideal and immortal.

Plotinus taught about the existence of a "ONE" existing eternally, representing absolute Perfection and Beauty, who could be defined as the force without which nothing could exist. The "ONE" consists of Reason and Matter and the less perfect creature takes its light from the more perfect, so that all creatures take their light from the "ONE".

The above said leads us to conclude that the Bible and the Koran cannot be literally the words of God. The belief in such an idea is an offence to common sense and to reason given to us by God. As described in Chapter 6.H.1, certain Twelve Imami Muslim Shia scholars believe that the Koran was altered while assembling it, and that there were verses that were deleted and others added, as reported by Al-Tubrusi.

The Ismaili and Alawite Muslim Sects followers believe in an Gnostic (Batini) meaning of the Koran words: that the truth is hidden behind the apparent meaning of the Koran words, known only to Imams. While the Mu'tazila Muslim sect followers (Chapter 6.H.2a) declared that the Koran was created. They based their belief on reason, and said that by using reason a person could differentiate between bad and good without relying on the Koranic text.

Christian Churches have already agreed that the Evangels are not the literal words of God, although inspired by Him. So it remains for the Sunni Muslim authorities to join some Shia Muslim sects and Christian Churches and reach a similar conclusion.

There is a definite possibility for peaceful coexistence between Christianity and Islam if both strive to interpret the Bible and the Koran basing their interpretation on reason and logic, not adhering to the punctual and literal meaning of the text but to its spirit and purpose, and when required to delete the incorrect insertions.

As we cannot accept Moses's Law with its notion that the Israeli people are God's chosen people, its rule on slavery, usury, payment of tribute, abusive divorce of women, retribution, stoning, burning and killing apart from the Ten Commandments of God, as clarified in Chapter 5 B, similarly we cannot accept the Koran's Sharia and other Koran rules in the twenty-first century covering: wars of conquest in Allah's name, the notion that the Muslim Nation is the best nation, killing the apostate, payment of tribute by non-Muslims, plunder of women, slavery, polygamy, beating of women, inequality between men and women in tribunals and inheritance, lashing adulterers, cutting off hands and feet and stoning.

Continuing to be strict into interpreting and performing literally the Koran words will lead in time to further backwardness of Muslim people. Extremism and terror will backfire and will destroy its initiators.

Now that transmission of ideas and news became widespread through printing techniques, audio visual means and the internet, each person is capable on his own to read the Bible and the Koran and form his own opinion from the original sources, without having to rely on the interpretation of early centuries Christian Church Fathers, and their Muslim counterparts, who in their time were counted on single hand fingers due to scarcity of educated men. Ignorance is the main cause of human misery.

Written laws historically proceeded from the Code of Laws of Hammurabi (a human made law) as per Chapter 1, followed by Moses' Law, the Roman Law, Justinian's Law, the Koran's Sharia Law and ended in our epoch with state constitutions of different countries and the Universal Declaration of Human Rights. Regarding Christianity, Jesus Christ abrogated Moses' Law and taught his disciples to follow only its spirit, abolishing many beliefs held by the Rabbis and denounced their practices as in (Luke 11: 46-52: "And he said: Woe also to you scholars of the law! You impose on people burdens hard to carry, but you yourselves do not lift one finger to touch them... You have taken away the key of knowledge. You yourselves did not enter and you stopped those trying to enter."), and concentrated on ethical behaviour, love, tolerance and respect of the other as in (Matthew 7: 12 "So whatever you wish that men would do to you, do so to them; for this is the Law and the prophets") and taught that all men are brothers in humanity. He separated the spiritual (the spiritual beliefs of a person) from state laws, which vary in time and place.

CONCLUSION

To answer the main subject of this book, about the possibility of Christians and Muslims to coexist peacefully, and from the above exposed analysis, we deduce that this is possible on condition that a new examination of the present day existing texts of the Old and New Testament and the Koran are made to discern what could have been inspired by God and what has been added by men, due to memory failures as these texts were written many years after the death of their authors, due to inaccurate and basic skills in writing and translation, hand copying techniques over many centuries, and the personal interpretation of the Scriptures.

Also, removing the sanctity of the religious texts is the key to their understanding. Believers should read with an open mind the Bible and the Koran in order to understand their meaning, away from old and early centuries interpretations made by rabbis, clerics and imams.

We should use Reason given to us by God to try to reach the truth. Any texts referring to God's orders to kill and or discriminate between people because of their race, ethnicity and religious beliefs should be discarded as false, as well as any ordering to kill and persecute people in His name, including any trade in slaves and human beings. Also should be discarded as false any texts suggesting that the acts of men, bad or good being commanded and created by God.

God who gave us our conscience and reason has given us a perfect tool, which we have to use to differentiate between false and true, bad and good. God, who is all Goodness, cannot be the initiator of some commands present in Moses' Law and the Koran's Sharia. And as Plato wrote in Chapter 3 above, wisdom is the knowledge of what is right and that a good act is good because it is useful to us in our efforts to be better and happier people and that ethics are not a matter of following blindly the scriptures for what is good or bad, but rather acting according to our Conscience and Reason.

The search for God by contemporary men continues, and the development of religious thought cannot stop. God was found by humans using Reason, and in knowledge resides the correct belief.

REFERENCES

- *The Code of Hammurabi* (Robert W. Rogers, New York 1917).
- The Avalon Project – Documents In Law, History & Diplomacy – *The Code of Hammurabi*, Translated by L.W. King.
- *The Republic* (η πολιτεια) (Plato, translated by Desmond Lee 2003).
- *The Bible* as per the ESV (English Standard Version).
- *The meaning of the Glorious Qur'an* (translated by Muhammad Marmaduke Picktahll 1970).
- *Futuh Al-Buldan* (Imam Abi Al-Abbass Ahmad Al-Balaziri, Al-Ma'aref Institution 1987 Beyrouth).
- The Introduction of Abd Al-Rahman Ibn Khaldoun (Dar Al-Jil Beyrouth).
- *History of Syria* (Philip K. Hitti, Macmillan Company, New York 1951).
- *Les Schismes dans L'Islam* (Henri Laoust Payot, Paris 1983).
- *Arab Christianity and its developments* (Dr. Salwa Belhaj Saleh – Dar Al-Taliaa, Beyrouth 1997).
- *Covert movements in the Muslim World* (Mohammad A. Al-Khatib, Amman Jordan 1986).
- *Histoire et religion des Nosairis* (Rene Dussaud, Librairie Emile Bouillon, Paris).
- *The encyclopaedia of the Antiochian Patriarchate,* 1st Volume Junieh, Lebanon 1997 (Father Dimitri Athanasiou).

- *History of religious thought of the Church Fathers* (bishop Kyrilos Salim Pesters, Father Hanna Alfakhouri, Father Joseph Alabsi Alboulisi, The Catholic Press, Lebanon 2001).
- *Herodotus, the Histories*, Aubrey de Selincourt/A.R. Burn, 1979 The Penguin Classics.
- *Les Croisades* Zoe Oldenbourg, Éditions Gallimard 1965.
- *Byzantium* (John Julius Norwich, Penguin Books 1993).

CPSIA information can be obtained
at www.ICGtesting.com
Printed in the USA
BVHW031035161122
651979BV00023B/291